THE WORLD OF
DOGS

Old English or Bobtail Sheepdog

HAMLYN
LONDON / NEW YORK / SYDNEY / TORONTO

THE WORLD OF DOGS

WENDY BOORER

Film actress Sophia Loren with her
white Poodle

Published by THE HAMLYN PUBLISHING GROUP LIMITED
LONDON · NEW YORK · SYDNEY · TORONTO
Hamlyn House, Feltham, Middlesex, England
© 1969   The Hamlyn Publishing Group Limited
Reprinted 1970, 1971, 1972
Printed in Italy by Arnoldo Mondadori Editore, Verona
ISBN 0 600 03975 7

CONTENTS

THE POPULARITY POLL

When the Kennel Club was founded in England in 1873 it recognised and registered forty breeds. Now as many as 110 breeds are registered. In some of these breeds so few animals are registered annually that they are always in danger of vanishing altogether. Many other breeds register a few hundred annually and have a steady and devoted following of enthusiasts. From this group a few breeds seem to catch the public's imagination, and become immensely fashionable. They are bred in their thousands before they decline in numbers again as their popularity wanes.

There are many guesses as to why a breed becomes fashionable but none are completely convincing. It has been suggested that to become fashionable a breed must be distinctive enough to be easily recognisable by the layman, and it must also have a certain amount of glamour about it. Certainly incidental patronage, which helps to get a breed recognised by a large section of the public, helps a great deal. The numbers of

King Charles Spaniels
at a show in 1910

These two Collies seem determined to be Top of the Pops again as they were in 1900

In 1910 Pomeranians rivalled
Pekinese in popularity

Corgis increased when they were known to be Royal favourites. Disney's film '101 Dalmations' increased the registration figures of that breed, and current advertising campaigns are popularising both the Old English Sheepdog and the Basset Hound. Reasons for the decline of a very fashionable breed are more obvious. As well as the fact that fashion is fickle, a number of people will be attracted to the breed by the chance to make money. Where a large number of puppies are turned out solely with the idea of a quick profit, quality in both health and temperament is liable to decline.

In 1900 Collies, both Rough and Smooth, were the top dogs in Britain. The boom in Collies had started some twenty years earlier and by 1900, £100 was considered a ridiculously low price for a show Collie. A number of Collies changed hands at over £1,000, particularly for export to America, where the boom was just starting. The top dog in America at this time was the English Setter. Indeed when the American Kennel Club published its first Stud Book in 1878, the first registration listed was the English Setter, Adonis. In Britain Smooth Fox Terriers, Irish Terriers and Bulldogs were also very popular.

By 1910 the Rough Collie had reached the top in America, though the decline had set in in Britain. Bulldogs, Pomeranians and Pekinese were popular in Britain. Large numbers of Smooth-haired Fox Ter-

From 1880 to 1900 Collies were the favourite dogs in Britain

The Wire-haired Fox Terrier (shown here in the pet clip) topped the charts in 1920

riers were bred but the Wire-haired variety was beginning to catch up, and by 1920 had ousted the Smooths from the top of the charts. Wire Fox Terriers remained very fashionable for two decades, even though they require a good deal of trimming to retain the smart appearance that caught the public's fancy in the first place. Pekinese, Bulldogs, Pomeranians and Airedale Terriers were all in the forefront in the 1920s, while in America Boston Terriers were all the rage. Bostons are an American breed created by a Mr Hopkin in Massachusetts in the 1870s. Alert and clean cut in appearance, they are one of the few smooth-coated dogs to have achieved top popularity.

Though Wire Fox Terriers were still at the top in 1930, they were being closely followed by the breed that was soon to usurp their position, the Cocker Spaniel. Alsatians were also popular. They had been brought to Britain from Germany after the First World War, chiefly by ex-servicemen who had been impressed by their intelligence. Because the name German Shepherd Dog was believed to prejudice the public against them at that time, they were called Alsatians instead. It is under the former name that they became top dog in America in the 1930s.

During the 1940s and 1950s Spaniels came to the fore on both sides

The Boston Terrier is a very smart and popular American breed

The Poodle has been the most popular pet during the 1960s

Sitting pretty for a
fashionable future?

The Royal Family's fondness for Corgis boosted
the breed's popularity with the public

What will it be, Sir, shave or haircut?

Top dog in the U.S.A. for
seventeen years was
the American Cocker Spaniel

of the Atlantic. In Britain it was the Cocker Spaniel, whose silky coat
and merry and affectionate character endeared him to all. In America
it was the American Cocker Spaniel. This breed had the distinction of
being at the top in the American Kennel Club registrations for seventeen
years (1936 to 1952), longer than any other breed. The American Cocker
has descended from the English Cocker but is slightly smaller with a
rounded skull and a much more profuse coat. Numbers of this breed
have recently been imported into Britain and have begun to make their
mark in the show ring.

By the 1960s Poodles were the most numerous breed in both countries.
Poodles come in three sizes, Standard, Miniature and Toy, and it was
the last two that made great strides forward. Poodles are clever, lively
little dogs that come in an attractive variety of colours. The need to
have them clipped regularly and the desire to dress them up led to a
great boom in dog beauty parlours and dog accessories.

The latest registration figures show that Poodles are still at the top
in America but their numbers are declining in Britain. In 1967 more
than 14,000 Alsatians were registered in Britain, and as they are popular in many other countries too they may well claim to head the
world popularity poll.

We may be mongrels but we
are pretty popular too

Alsatians may well be the most
popular breed in the world today

Statistics tend to show that though the dog population is decreasing,
the proportion of pedigree dogs to mongrels is steadily rising. It would
be foolish to predict which breed will steal the limelight from the Alsatian. Labrador Retrievers are not so far behind them in numbers,
and Yorkshire Terriers are in third place. Over 1,200 of these were
exported to the United States in 1967 — so possibly they are the breed
all set for the fashionable future.

WILD DOGS

There are a number of theories about the origin of the domestic dog and it is doubtful if we shall ever know for certain exactly how it evolved. All the diverse types of domestic dog, from the St. Bernard to the Chihuahua, from the Greyhound to the Bulldog, have been created by selective breeding. If we go back to the Neolithic and Middle Stone Ages we find the bones of the first domestic dogs. These were medium-sized animals, and were probably still scavengers that were neither bred nor fed purposely by man. Where these primitive dogs came from is a question that cannot be answered with certainty, but a close look at the domestic dog's nearest wild relatives provides some clues.

The family Canidae to which the dog belongs contains thirty-six other species, which include the wolves, jackals, and foxes. Despite many popular stories, there is no scientific evidence that a cross between a dog and a fox has ever been produced. The anatomical differences between the two are many and, in addition, the gestation period of the fox is much shorter than that of the dog.

There is very much stronger evidence to suggest that the wolf and the dog are very closely related. Many anatomical features, particularly the teeth, are identical, and wolves and dogs interbreed with no difficulty, given the opportunity. The Eskimos are supposed to have taken advantage of this to improve the stamina of their sledge dogs, by staking out their bitches in season away from their encampments, in order to attract the attention of male wolves.

Wolves are found in North America, Europe and Asia, but were even more widely distributed in the past. The last ones in the British Isles were exterminated in Ireland in the eighteenth century. An adult male wolf may stand thirty inches at the shoulder and weigh 100 pounds. However, size and coat differ slightly according to the area from which the animal comes, and colour ranges from grey to tawny. Wolves, like dogs, are social animals, and they run in packs made up of family groups. Within the pack a remarkable degree of co-operation is shown during the hunt. One animal will cut out an old or weak member of a herd of deer or elk, and other members of the pack will take turns in running it down. Wolf cubs, if taken young enough, can be tamed quite easily and they can also be taught to bark, something that they do not do in the wild. Some of the more primitive types of dog, including some sledge dogs and the Basenji, also do not bark but express themselves by a variety of yelps, howls and yodelling noises.

The wolf is probably the closest relative of the domestic dog

The coyote is only found in North America, where it is still quite common on the prairies and the plains, despite being extensively hunted by man. The behaviour of coyotes is very similar to that of wolves but the animals themselves are only about half the size, weighing about forty pounds when adult. The coyote feeds on small mammals and thus can live in semi-desert country which would not support a wolf pack. Persecution by man has caused the adaptable coyote to change its habits. Once they were pack animals but now are often solitary scavengers outside the mating and rearing season. The coyote has achieved a certain notoriety because of the cunning with which it avoids man's traps and because of the complexity and resonance of its howl. Two coyotes singing can sound like many times that number. The gestation period is the same as for the dog, but the coyote has never seriously been considered an ancestor of the domestic dog, because most of the evidence suggests that the dog was first domesticated in the Middle East, while the coyote is only found in North America.

There are four species of jackal inhabiting Africa and southern Asia. They are all closely related but differ markedly in colouring. Now they are mainly solitary animals, scavenging at the kills of larger carnivores, eating carrion and killing small mammals for themselves. Like most of

The coyote is still quite
common on the
North American prairies

There is no evidence that a cross between a dog and a fox
has ever been produced. These two are just good friends

the wild dogs they are nocturnal in habit. Occasionally small packs of jackals hunt together, and it is believed that in the past they were pack animals and that the advance of civilisation made them change their habits. The jackal is about the size of the coyote and will interbreed with both dogs and wolves. Some authorities believe that primitive man first adopted the scavenging jackal as a useful camp follower; and that when these tribes migrated north, they took with them jackal-like dogs which interbred with the more northerly wolves. Against this theory is the fact that jackals do not show as many dog-like habits as the wolf; there are possibly some differences in the structure of the teeth; and jackals are much more odoriferous animals than either dogs or wolves.

The scientific name for the domestic dog is *Canis familiaris*, and included in the genus *Canis* are both the Dingo and the New Guinea Singing Dog. The Dingo is the only large mammal native to Australia that is not a marsupial. It is believed therefore that the Dingo did not originate in Australia but sailed there as a half-domesticated companion of the aboriginal settlers and later reverted to the wild. The Dingo is reddish fawn in colour and often has white paws, a white patch on the chest and a white tip to the tail. This type of white marking is more common in domesticated animals than wild ones. Black and cream coloured specimens also occur. They are about twenty inches high, and interbreed readily with the domestic dog. They also do not bark in the wild, but

Silverback jackal in
Amboseli National Park, Kenya

Coyotes are nowadays mainly solitary in their habits

25

when caught young and tamed they will learn to do so.

The Dingo is now a major pest in Australia. Although they do destroy a large number of wild rabbits and other small mammals, the Dingos' main food is sheep. Being naturally alert, suspicious and cunning animals, they have been able to survive in a country where the farmers have tried to kill them all off.

The New Guinea Singing Dog looks very similar to the Dingo and is also believed to have been brought to New Guinea by the original settlers. Little is known about its habits in the wild, though its name comes from its remarkable howling cry. Finally mention must be made of pariah dogs. These are semi-wild dogs found in countries bordering the Mediterranean, throughout the Middle East, and southwards through the Malay Archipelago to Japan. Usually medium-sized animals, they vary in colouring and structure, and have been classified into five distinct types. They are nearly always scavengers, living on the outskirts of human settlements, and they vary in temperament from the completely wild to the semi-tame. Adults caught in the wild can be tamed and trained successfully, and puppies reared by humans behave like domesticated dogs. They interbreed readily with the imported European breeds and, because of this, the recognisable pariah types may soon disappear. Though they do not always live in packs, pariahs sharing the same territory will band together to rout a common enemy. When domesticated the pariah makes a very good watch-dog, being naturally suspicious and alert. It is also loyal and devoted and exceptionally hardy, as its background makes it highly resistant to disease. Where the pariah dog came from is still a puzzle. It is claimed by some that, when the ancient civilisations of the Middle East declined and vanished, the domesticated dogs of the region reverted to the wild. This would

The New Guinea Native or Singing Dog is named for its strange howling cry

The Dingo runs wild in Australia, though pups are tamed by the Aborigines and used for hunting

account for the diversity of types that are found. Another theory is that pariahs are descended from some primitive dog, rather like the Dingo in appearance, and that they represent a transition stage between a truly wild dog and the domesticated variety. The theories are not mutually exclusive, though irrefutable proof for either has not yet been found.

BREED EVOLUTION

A rise in the standard of living of a country is paralleled by a growth in the sale of pedigree puppies. People not only want a dog as a companion but also as something they can be proud of. By choosing a particular breed people can get the shape, the colour and the type of coat that they prefer in a dog. The discerning can also get the type of temperament they prefer, for though it is true that a dog's character is mainly formed by its upbringing, temperamental differences do occur between different breeds. Those who like one-man dogs, aloof with all strangers, can choose accordingly. Someone who likes a bold, aggressive dog can select a breed where a typical specimen is likely to have these characteristics. Some breeds are better with children than others. Some breeds have an affectionate, sentimental character; others have an independent, impudent attitude to life and authority. The choice is very wide and should be made with care.

In Britain 110 breeds are recognised by the Kennel Club. The American Kennel Club recognises 132 and there are probably well over 350 breeds in the world altogether. This enormous diversity is due to two things; the tendency of *Canis familiaris* towards variation, and the ability of man to fix these aberrations by selective breeding. The ability to reproduce its desirable qualities in its offspring is the advantage that the pure-bred dog has over the mongrel. It is this guarantee of a certain level of quality in pure-bred puppies that leads police forces and other bodies using trained dogs in quantity, to use specialised breeds for their purpose. There seems no foundation in fact for the popular belief that mongrels are more intelligent than pedigree animals. There is, however, some evidence to suggest that they may be healthier. This is due to a number of factors. Selective breeding will stabilise undesirable qualities as well as desirable ones, and sometimes these are extremely difficult to breed out without destroying the type of dog that is required. The law of the survival of the fittest applies to some extent to mongrel puppies, whereas pure-bred puppies have a commercial value and special attention will be given to the weak ones to ensure that they survive. Some breeds too have very exaggerated conformation. It is obvious that if an animal is required to have a large head and a small pelvis, whelping is liable to be unnaturally difficult. Again, breeds with very pushed-in faces are more liable to respiratory troubles and heart attacks.

The show ring is the place where the dog breeders' skill is judged. Each breed has a written standard describing the ideal that everyone should

The Old English Sheepdog is quite an ancient breed

Dogs arriving with their
owners for the International
Dog Show at Islington in 1865

be aiming for in that breed. Breed standards, being written by fallible humans, vary widely in quality. Some breeds have a perfunctory outline from which to work, others a verbose blueprint. The written word of course, means something slightly different to each person who reads it, which is one of the reasons why the same dog does not win all the time.

Ideally health, temperament and conformation should all be taken into account when judging a dog. Unfortunately, too often it is only the latter which is taken into consideration. Also there is no way in the show ring

of assessing working ability. The fact that the dog's shape is an ideal one for the work it is meant to do is no guarantee that it has the mental qualities necessary. This is not so important in breeds whose original function has long ceased to exist, but it leads to an unfortunate dichotomy in such animals as gun-dogs. There are liable to be two distinct types of these: the working dog, whose looks are unimportant, and the show specimen, whose working ability is suspect or non-existent. Some attempts have been made to bridge the gap by the ruling that a gun-dog cannot claim the full title of Champion without having proved its merit at a Field Trial. This is not wholly successful, as many owners do not have the time, ability or inclination to both work and show their dogs.

Most pure-bred dogs had in the past a working function; they were bred to do a particular job. Sometimes their creation was rather haphazard. A particular locality might produce a dog whose vermin-killing exploits achieved local fame. This animal would tend to be used as a sire, and in this way a strain of dogs related in looks and working ability might be created in the neighbourhood. Other breeds were the creation of an individual who wanted a dog for a specific purpose and who was not satisfied with what was locally available. In Wales in the 1850s, Captain Edwardes created the Sealyham Terrier for badger-baiting. At the same period in Birmingham, Mr James Hinks was producing by judi-

The Bearded Collie was in danger of dying out but is now steadily increasing its following

cious crossing the white Bull Terrier. He wanted a fighting dog that would combine agility with power. The Dobermann Pinscher takes its name from Louis Dobermann who founded the breed in Germany in the 1890s. These were dogs bred specifically to be good guards.

Types of dog whose working function disappears are liable to die out. There is a long list of breeds that have gone completely in the last 100 years of so. It includes the White English Terrier, The Black and Tan Old English Terrier, the Blue Paul, the Scottish Spaniel, the Norfolk Spaniel and probably the Welsh Grey Sheepdog. Here the show ring can perform a useful function because, if enough people become interested in exhibiting a breed whose working function has ended, that type of dog is no longer in danger of dying out. One recent example of this is the Bearded Collie. Shaggy sheepdogs of this type have been known in Scotland since the sixteenth century at least. They are believed to have been brought there from Poland and Russia by ships engaged in the Baltic trade. They were used for working sheep and later for cattle droving. By the beginning of this century they were scarce. Railway transportation had diminished the need for cattle droving dogs and the Border Collie had become the premier sheep working breed. Few were left by the end of the Second World War and it is entirely due to the efforts and determination of Mrs G. O. Willison that they did not die out altogether. She founded her kennel with the bitch Jeannie of Bothkennar, and campaigned the Kennel Club for breed recognition. In 1959 there were enough Bearded Collies for Challenge Certificates to be awarded, and since then the breed has slowly and steadily increased its following.

The Kennel Club decides whether to recognise a breed as pure-bred according to the evidence put before it. This may consist of proof, as in the case of the Bearded Collie, of the existence of that type of dog for a considerable period of time. Alternatively, proof may be required that the dog is regarded as pure-bred in its country of origin. The Pekinese is one such foreign breed. These toy dogs had been bred in the Peking Palace for the Emperors of China for many centuries. In conformation they were meant to resemble the Buddhist Lion and they were not only carefully bred, but carefully guarded and highly valued. When the British sacked the Summer Palace in Peking in 1860, five of these small dogs were found alive and brought to England. Only the pair in the possession of the Duke of Richmond produced any offspring, and it is from these, and from a handful that were smuggled out during the next forty years, that all the present day Pekinese are descended. It is salutary for those who completely condemn inbreeding to remember the large number of breeds that started this way with very few individuals.

For a breed to be allotted breed classes with Challenge Certificates at a Championship Show, it must have registered more than 150 specimens with the Kennel Club during the preceding three years. Undoubtedly more breeds will be added to the Kennel Club's recognised list, but probably much more slowly than in the past. People creating new breeds would not receive any encouragement from the ruling body of the canine world. One type of dog that is on the increase in Britain and perhaps

Hard to say who feels hotter, the Boxer or his master, at this dog show in the U.S.S.R.

The Pekinese was for centuries exclusively bred for the Emperors of China

may finally require recognition is the Jack Russell Terrier. In the early nineteenth century, Parson Jack Russell built up a strain of wire-haired terriers to run with his hounds on Exmoor. This strain died out but the name lingered on. Now the Jack Russell Terrier is a short-legged animal, predominantly white with black or tan patches and with a tail docked about half way. Though they can have prick or drop ears and smooth, wire or broken coats, they are still a recognisable and increasingly popular little dog. They may yet make the twenty-first breed of terrier to be created in Great Britain.

The Jack Russell Terrier has not yet received official recognition

A much decorated champion
Collie in the Soviet Union

Two sad Beagles awaiting recognition

PEARLS DROPPED FROM THE LIPS OF HER IMPERIAL MAJESTY TZU HSI, DOWAGER EMPRESS OF THE FLOWERY LAND OF CONFUCIUS.

Let the Lion Dog be small; let it wear the swelling cape of dignity around its neck; let it display the billowing standard of pomp over its back.

Let its face be black; let its forefront be shaggy; let its forehead be straight and low, like unto the brow of a boxer.

For its colour, let it be that of the lion — a golden sable, to be carried in the sleeve of a yellow robe, or the colour of a red bear, or of a black bear or a white bear, or striped like a dragon, so that there may be dogs appropriate to every costume in the Imperial wardrobe, whose fitness to appear at public ceremonies and functions shall be judged by their colour and their artistic contrast with the Imperial robes.

Let it venerate its ancestors, and deposit offerings in the Canine Cemetery of the Forbidden City on each new moon.

Let it be taught to refrain from gadding about; let it comport itself with the dignity of a duchess; let it learn to bite the foreign devils instantly.

Let it wash its face like a cat with its paws; let it be dainty in its food that it shall be known for a royal and imperial dog by its fastidiousness.

Let its eyes be large and luminous; let its ears be set like the sails of a war-junk; let its nose be like that of the monkey-god of the Hindus.

Let its forelegs be bent so that it shall not desire to wander far or leave the Imperial precincts.

Let its body be shaped like that of a hunting lion spying for its prey.

Let its feet be tufted with plentiful hair that its footfalls may be noiseless; and for its standard of pomp let it rival the whisk of the Tibetan yak, which is flourished to protect the Imperial litter from the attacks of flying insects.

Let it be lively that it may afford entertainment by its gambols; let it be wary that it may not involve itself in danger, let it be sociable in its habits that it may live in amity with the other beasts, fishes or birds that find protection in the Imperial Palace.

A Chinese Emperor's Ice Chest surmounted by a Lion Dog

TERRIERS

Although the Bulldog is claimed as the British national breed, in many ways the terriers are more truly representative of Great Britain. Of the twenty-two terrier breeds recognised by the English and American Kennel Clubs, only one did not originate in these islands. The history of terriers is not well documented for they were bred as vermin killers, dogs to bolt the fox and the badger from their earths, and as such they did not attract the attention of the literate and the aristocratic. Their name comes from the French 'la terre' and indicates that their main function has always been to go to earth. Though the first reference to terriers is not found in literature until the fourteenth century, a Roman bronze carving found in Northumberland of a short-legged, rough-coated dog indicates that the type was known much earlier.

As a group the terriers are the extroverts of the canine world. They are lively, fun-loving and hardy. Their courage, independence of spirit, and gaiety ensure that they will always have plenty of admirers.

The Airedale Terrier is the largest of the group, being roughly twenty-three inches at the shoulder. They originated around Bingley in Yorkshire and are good water dogs. The hard, wiry coat should be black and tan and needs some trimming. Airedales are usually patient and gentle with children, and are tractable enough to have been used extensively for police and war work in Germany.

The Bedlington Terrier has a deceptively mild appearance. The fastest of the terriers, it was originally a gipsies' dog which attracted the attention of the Northumbrian miners, who used it for ratting and racing. The Bedlington's coat should be thick and linty, and either light blue or pale fawn in colour. They need a considerable amount of trimming to leave the pronounced and distinctive topknot. Lovable and gentle towards the human race, they can be jealous of other dogs and are redoubtable fighters.

The Border Terrier is still very much a working terrier. It is both big enough to follow a horse and small enough to bolt a fox. The most usual colour is red or wheaten and the harsh, dense coat needs no trimming. As the name implies, this terrier originally came from the Scottish Border country and it is probably one of the oldest terrier breeds. They possess a great deal of charm and their coat needs little attention to keep it tidy. Being strong, active dogs they need rather more exercise than their size would suggest.

The Bull Terrier is known as the gladiator of the canine race. Descended

Keenly alert, the Cairn Terrier has a fearless and gay disposition

1 Border Terrier
2 Bedlington Terrier
3 Airedale Terrier

from a long line of fighting dogs, the Bull Terrier is a muscular, powerful animal that needs a certain amount of firm handling. They are courageous to the point of rashness and make good guard dogs. This is also one of the breeds that is excellent with children. They are dogs of individuality that inspire a passionate devotion in their owners. The all white Bull Terrier was first bred by Mr Hinks of Birmingham in the 1860s. The white ones were then much more refined than the coloured specimens, but now both are even in quality. In America the white and coloured varieties are classified and shown separately, but in England they compete against each other in the show ring.

The Miniature Bull Terrier is recognised as a separate breed in Great

Britain. They should be exact replicas of the larger variety, but the height must be not more than fourteen inches and the weight not more than twenty pounds.

The Cairn Terrier is one of the older Scottish breeds and probably played a part in the making of both the Scottish Terrier and the West Highland White Terrier. They are shaggy in appearance with a hard weatherproof outer coat which requires little trimming. They are usually grey or brindled and are expected to have a fearless and gay disposition. They are passionate hunters of small game.

The Dandie Dinmont Terrier is a dog with a very distinctive and engaging appearance. The large, dark, melting eyes and the soft white topknot belie the stubborn, independent character. Dandie Dinmonts can trace their history back to the 1700s and acquired both name and fame by being mentioned by Sir Walter Scott in his novel 'Guy Mannering'. Though aloof with strangers, the Dandie is an affectionate family dog, albeit one who prefers to please himself rather than his master. The colour should be either pepper, which is bluish black to light silvery grey, or mustard, which is reddish brown to pale fawn.

There are two varieties of Fox Terrier, the Smooth-haired and the Wire-haired. The only difference between them is one of coat, the Smooth variety having a straight, flat, dense coat while the Wires have a jacket like coconut matting. This coat requires a great deal of trimming if the dog is to look smart. Both varieties should stand about fifteen inches high and weigh about eighteen pounds. As their name suggests, these dogs were first of all hunt terriers, bred to follow the hounds and bolt the fox from its earth. They are predominantly white in colour to make them easily distinguishable from their quarry, and their tails are docked to three-quarter length, making a useful handle for a huntsman pulling them out of a hole. The modern Fox Terrier is still keen and lively in temperament, though a few individuals are too excitable and noisy to be ideal companions.

The Irish Terrier is another breed with a nickname. Known as the 'Dare Devils' or the 'Red Devils', Irish Terriers combine a remarkable sweetness towards the human race with rather an aggressive attitude towards the canine one. Their coat should be hard and wiry, and any

1 Bull Terrier
2 Cairn Terrier

1

2

1 Lakeland Terrier
2 Irish Terrier
3 Dandie Dinmont Terrier
4 Kerry Blue Terrier
5 Manchester Terrier
6 Smooth-haired Fox Terrier
7 Wire-haired Fox Terrier

shade of red is acceptable, provided the dog is whole-coloured.

Another courageous terrier from Ireland is the Kerry Blue. Kerry Blues have the typical terrier's attitude to life, being game, independent dogs with the ability to enjoy every situation to the full. Their coats should be plentiful, soft and wavy. Any colour of blue is acceptable, but this colour does not show through until the animal is about eighteen months of age, puppies being born black. The coat needs considerable trimming with scissors, but Kerry Blues have the advantage of single rather than double coats, which means that considerably less hair is shed around the house.

The Lakeland Terrier has developed from the hunt terriers that accompanied the packs of fell hounds in the English Lake District. Reasonnably long in the leg and narrow in the chest, the Lakeland could creep into the narrow rocky crevices favoured by the hill foxes, and also jump and climb the screes with the hounds. Their colour is usually black and tan, or red. Their coat is harsh and needs trimming, and their appearance is described as 'workmanlike'. They are not so quarrelsome as some of the other terrier breeds.

Manchester Terriers and Bull Terriers are the only members of this group with smooth coats. The Manchester is a black and tan dog and the richness of the colour, the placing of the tan markings, and the clear division between the two colours, are all important points in the show ring. Originally Black and Tan Terriers, of a type now extinct, were used in the rat pits and for rabbit coursing. These, crossed with Whippets, produced fast, game dogs from which the modern Manchester Terrier is descended. This terrier's sleek, glossy appearance should make it more popular.

The Norfolk and the Norwich Terriers are similar to each other in appearance and ancestry except for the carriage of the ears. The Norfolk has a dropped ear and the Norwich an erect one. The British Kennel Club allowed the two varieties to become separate breeds in 1964, but in America they are all known as Norwich Terriers. These are lovable little dogs with steady, affectionate temperaments. They stand about ten inches at the shoulder and are usually red or wheaten in colour. The

5

6

7

1 Norfolk Terrier
2 Norwich Terrier
3 Skye Terrier

hard, wiry coat should not be trimmed. In contrast to the short hair on the head, the longer, harsher coat on the neck and shoulders almost forms a mane.

The Scottish Terrier has been claimed by its supporters to be the oldest of the Scottish breeds. It seems more likely however that all small dogs bred to go to earth after vermin were called Scottish Terriers. Not until the nineteenth century were the differences between the various types accentuated by breeders, and the Cairn, West Highland White and Scottish Terrier produced. The Scottish Terrier is an individualist that has always had many admirers on both sides of the Atlantic. The coat needs trimming if the dog is to look smart. Besides the almost universal black, wheaten and brindle colours are also permissible. Unfortunately the breed standard demands a body shape which makes whelping difficult.

The Sealyham Terrier was the creation of a Captain J. Edwardes, who

1

1 Sealyham Terrier
2 Welsh Terrier
3 Scottish Terrier

2

3

45

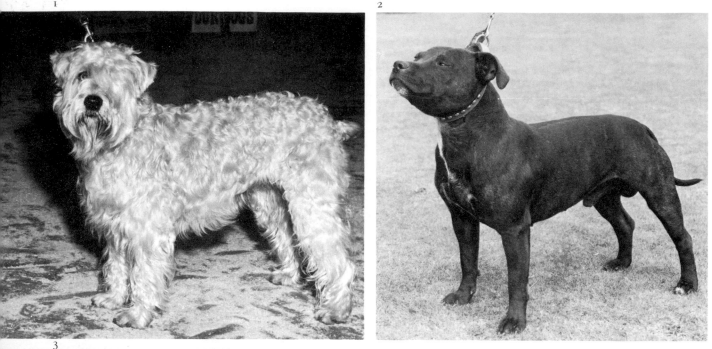

1 Soft-coated Wheaten Terrier
2 Staffordshire Bull Terrier
3 West Highland White Terrier

from 1850 onwards strove to produce a short-legged terrier that would tackle anything from a polecat to a badger. Quite what he used to get the result he wanted is a matter for conjecture, but we do know he was pretty ruthless in his methods of culling those he considered not courageous enough. The Sealyham took its name from Captain Edwardes's estate. Today they are kept mainly as pets, being good guards and amusing companions.

The Skye Terrier enjoyed great popularity until the early years of this century. It has a well authenticated history going back four centuries, and it appeared in quite large numbers at the earliest dog shows. Their decline in numbers may have been due to the length of their coat or to a certain surliness that became apparent. The latter has now been bred out, though Skyes still remain one-man dogs.

The Soft-coated Wheaten Terrier is not recognised in America and not well known in Britain. The Irish Kennel Club recognised them as a distinct breed in 1937 and as a National breed in 1939. They are hardy and affectionate animals with no exaggerations of conformation. The coat should be silky with light, loose curls, and requires no trimming. The colour should be wheaten, though puppies are born a reddish colour which later changes to the correct shade.

The Staffordshire Bull Terrier is quite closely akin to the type of dog that fought for its living in the days before organised dog fights became an illegal sport. With such a background, it is not suprising that Staffordshire Bull Terriers are as tough and tenacious as they come. They are friendly dogs with people but should not be owned by those who cannot or will not train them in restraint towards other dogs. The smooth coat can be practically any colour.

The Welsh Terrier appears to the uninitiated to be a slightly larger edition of the Lakeland, but the Welsh Terrier is always black and tan

Australian Terrier

and stands an inch or so higher at the shoulder. The head and the expression are the chief points of difference between the two. The Welsh Terrier is probably the nearest we have to the extinct black and tan, broken-haired Old English Terrier. Though like all terriers it is courageous and hardy, the Welsh Terrier is not usually aggressive.

There is evidence to suggest that a strain of white, short-legged terriers have been bred at Poltalloch in Scotland since the 1800s. The modern West Highland White Terrier is descended from these and is a gay, jaunty dog, deservedly very popular. The harsh, white outer coat picks up little dirt and needs little in the way of trimming.

Finally the one terrier recognised in Britain and America that did not originate in the British Isles in the Australian Terrier. This is one of the smallest of the working terriers and was first exhibited in Melbourne in 1885. The coat is harsh, about two inches long, and preferably blue with tan on the head and legs. They are affectionate dogs and rather quieter than some of the other terrier breeds.

BIZARRE DOGS

By selective breeding over many centuries man has produced some very odd dogs indeed. It is difficult to believe that the decorative spots of the Dalmation, the wrinkled head of the Bloodhound, the short legs of the Dachshund and the long stilts of the Borzoi have all been established by the patience and skill of generations of dog breeders — and that the common ancestor of all these types was probably a sandy, Dingo-like creature.

The more primitive of the dog breeds have certain distinguishing features. They do not normally bark, and bitches only come into season and are capable of breeding, once a year. Though there is wide variation among individuals, the females of most of the domesticated breeds of dog come into season twice a year. The breed that has recently gained a lot of publicity and many admirers is the barkless Basenji from the Congo. This is one of a number of African hunting dogs all very similar in build. They are certainly a very ancient type of dog, for Egyptian rock carvings show very similar animals — the prick ears and tightly curled tail being distinctive features. Basenjis were first imported succesfully into Britain in 1936, and since the Second World War have become increasingly popular. Though the Basenji does not bark, it is by no means a silent animal. It expresses itself by a series of yodels and yowls. Some of the sledge dog breeds also do not bark, making wolf-like howls instead. It is interesting that any individual dog reared in complete isolation will not bark unless taught to do so. Conversely, tame wolves reared in captivity can be taught to bark, though in the wild they would never do so.

Obviously the greatest variation achieved by dog breeders has been in size. The claim of the Chihuahua to be the smallest dog in the world cannot be denied. The origins of these diminutive dogs are unknown but they began to be imported into the United States from Mexico in the 1880s. Both smooth and long-coated varieties are recognised in Britain, and a dog two pounds in weight is no great rarity, though brood bitches must for obvious reasons be a good deal bigger. At the other end of the scale we have the really massive breeds like the St Bernard. One of these is reputed to have scaled eighteen stone. If we take height into consideration, the Irish Wolfhound is probably the tallest dog. The minimum height for the breed is thirty-one inches at the shoulder, and dogs of thirty-six inches are known. As well as having the size, weight and agility to tackle a wolf, the Wolfhound was expected to go into battle by the side of its master, and to be large and courageous enough to pull

Instead of barking, the Basenji makes a peculiar yodelling sound

A dog can sometimes be just too big for a guy to handle

The Greyhound is on average faster than any other dog

A wistful Chihuahua, the smallest breed in the world

It takes all sorts to make the canine world

the enemy from his horse.

Unfortunately the largest dogs do not have the longest lives and most big breeds are old by the time they reach nine years. On the whole toy dogs, though not the very tiny ones, are long lived — though perhaps too much depends on the treatment of the individual animal to generalize in this respect. Longevity records are notoriously difficult to prove. However there have been three recent well authenticated cases of dogs living to twenty-one years or thereabouts. In each of these cases the animal had been owned by the same family throughout its entire life. The breeds in question were a Curly-coated Retriever, a Border Terrier and a Samoyed. Another Border Terrier was claimed to have lived for twenty-eight years, but this dog had more than one owner and the story may well have got longer in the telling. In general most dogs are ageing at twelve years. Seventeen years is very old for a dog, though not remarkable. Some few individuals may achieve twenty or more.

The claim to be the fastest dog in the world is disputed between the Greyhound and the Saluki. A Saluki has been credited with a speed of forty-three miles per hour. The fastest British Greyhound was a dog

A bored St Bernard. This is one of the largest breeds of dog.

A Shih Tzu — hairy

Lhasa Apso — hairier

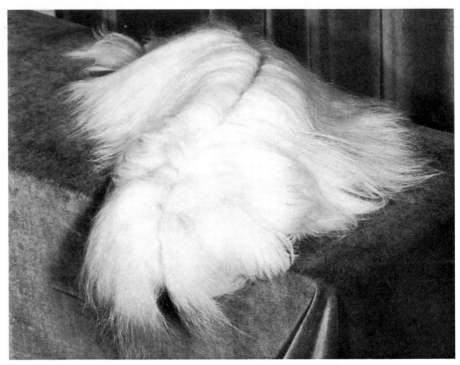

Maltese — hairiest

called Pigalle Wonder who clocked up over thirty-seven miles per hour. Dog racing is a popular sport in Germany and Holland, and of the various breeds used, the Greyhound is easily the fastest. Greyhounds average about thirty-four miles per hour on these continental tracks; the next fastest are Whippets averaging thirty-two miles per hour. Salukis, Borzois and Afghans are all slower.

The weirdest dogs with regard to looks are the hairless breeds. These seem to have originated in Africa, and they have always been rarities and highly prized. They were taken east along the trade routes to China, and west by the Spaniards trading with South America and Mexico in the seventeenth century. Being both rare and odd they were accredited with miraculous healing powers, and in Jamaica were known as 'fever dogs', being held next to the skin of the patient. Though their therapeutic effect may be doubted, they probably made very good hot water bottles as their normal temperature is some two to three degrees higher than that of any other breed. The Mexican Hairless Dog is now fairly well established in Mexico, and a few specimens are present in Britain. In size and structure it is rather like a Manchester Terrier and its skin can be bronze, grey or black. Some dogs are attractively mottled, though too much depigmentation is not considered desirable. The Mexican Kennel Club recognises a smaller variety with a height of about eleven inches and a weight of eleven pounds. These can be any colour including white,

And here are the least
hairy — the Chinese Crested ...

... and the Mexican Hairless

Two prize-winning
Poodles at a dog show
in the Soviet Union

blue or pink. There are also a few Chinese Crested Dogs in Britain. These too are small and naked, except for a mop of long hair on the skull and a tuft on the tail tip.

The greatest contrast to the hairless dogs is provided by the Hungarian Puli. This Hungarian Sheepdog has become quite popular in America since it was first imported in the 1930s. The dog has an immense amount of long, profuse coat which is fine in texture, so that it mats easily into long cords. Dog hair like this used to be widely used in the Baltic States and Russia; fine hair can be spun and used for clothing, while coarser hair is used for upholstery and making felt hats and boots. Most dog hair can be spun, by those who have the time and patience. During the First World War the combings from Pekinese were collected and spun and made into bedsocks and waistcoats for the wounded. The result was said to be comparable with camel for its softness and warmth. Sherpa Tensing wears clothing woven from the hair of his Lhasa Apso. Various breed enthusiasts wear Poodle jumpers, Samoyed sweaters and Old English Sheepdog jackets. All are claimed to be rather tickly.

Dogs have also been bred extensively for their skin and fur. In Britain in the seventeenth century dogskin was used for many things including hats and gloves. The Chow was bred in China for both fur and meat. Dog farms existed where Chows were reared to the age of nine or ten months and then killed and skinned. The pelts were sometimes exported under the name of 'China fur'.

54

In the past, dog flesh has been eaten in many parts of the world. In Africa, particularly in and around the Sudan, some tribes regarded their hunting dogs both as a means of catching food and as a food in themselves. In the Philippines, the Philippine Islands Dog was regarded as edible. Sunday morning dog markets were held where pariah dogs were sold for the table. Incidentally pariahs were scavengers and capable of transmitting a number of diseases to man. Usually dogs bred for the table were fed a cereal diet as this gave their flesh a more succulent flavour. The Maoris of New Zealand regarded their dogs as a sacrificial dish. Captain Cook ate a dish of Maori dog flesh in 1769 under the impression that it was freshly killed lamb. The Maoris also used the hair of their dogs for decorating their spears. In Japan the Akita was eaten, as well as having its skin used for such items as the scabbards of ceremonial swords.

The most widely known edible dog is of course, the Chow. There are a number of travellers' accounts of butchers' shops in Canton with dog carcasses hanging in rows, of the export of dog flesh from one part of China to another, and of dog flesh restaurants. The amount of nourishment to be obtained from a meal of dog flesh was believed to vary according to the colour of the dog's coat. Black dogs were supposed to provide more strength and also better fat for frying. These animals were reared and fattened on a cereal diet, and when the first Chows were imported into Britain many developed digestive troubles and skin diseases through being fed an all meat diet to which they were unaccustomed.

A skinned and gutted dog carcass hanging in a food market in Canton, southern China, in 1966

The most widely known edible breed is the Chow Chow, sometimes called the Cantonese Butcher-dog

55

FASHIONABLE DOGS

There is a tendency to think that the dog as a status symbol and a fashionable accessory is a relatively modern development. Nothing could be further from the truth. Ever since man began to breed dogs selectively some animals have been valued far more highly than their utilitarian worth. Along all the trade routes of the ancient world, dogs were taken as gifts for emperors and kings, and as valuable commodities for barter. Such animals not only received the best of care on the journey, being carried for instance in carts or on litters, but were also presented to their new owners with sumptuous accessories. The modern toy poodle wearing a plastic collar decorated with fake jewels is the end of a line of fashionable dogs stretching back to pre-history.

The dog collar itself has always been more than a means of restraint, being also a badge of ownership and an indication of rank. The excavations carried out at Pompeii (which was smothered by an eruption of Vesuvius in 79 AD) uncovered the skeleton of a dog stretched out beside that of a child. The dog had a silver collar with a Greek inscription saying that his name was 'Delta' and that he belonged to Severinus, whose life he had saved from a wolf. Silver was the favourite metal for collars, and the earliest travellers through Turkestan saw dogs 'the size of asses, and fierce as lions of Africa, which were led along in double chains covered with trappings of rich cloth and wearing silver collars and neckrings'. These were supposed to be the descendants of the dog of the Seven Sleepers who guarded his masters for three centuries and for this was rewarded with the joys of Mohammed's paradise.

Nearer home, the following list can be found entered in the inventory of the belongings of Henry VIII:
'VI dogge collars of crymson vellat wt.
VI lyhams of white leather.
Liame of white silk wt. a collar of white vellat embrawdered wt. perles, with swivel of silver.'
A lyham, or liame, was a lead and liam hounds were hounds which were hunted on a lead.

The German nobility of the seventeenth century valued their mastiffs highly. These were forerunners of the modern Great Dane, and the best of them wore collars of gold lined with velvet and engraved with their owner's initials. Lesser guard dogs wore silver collars.

The collar with spikes on the outside came into use very early on. The early sheep dogs were kept rather to protect the flocks than to help move

An Imperial aristocrat, bored with show business

The vogue for sentimental
greetings cards depicting dogs
began in Victorian times

Hark, the herald Poodle sings

58

Two happy aristocrats, cossetted and cared for

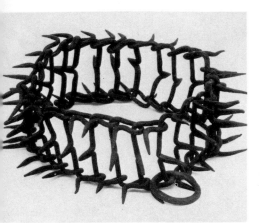

A late medieval dog collar,
probably used for boar hunting

This brass collar was engraved with its owner's address,
and dates from the 1860s

This early nineteenth century
kennel with its elaborate
stonework has been scheduled
as a building of special
architectural and historic interest

A lavish indoor kennel, lined
with velvet and satin, made for
Queen Marie Antoinette's lapdogs

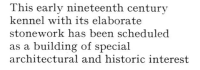

them. They wore heavy spiked collars to protect their throats from the attack of wolves. One such collar is on show in the London Museum and consists of a chain of wire links about three inches wide with three rows of inch-long spikes sticking out. Mrs. Biernoff who recently imported a pair of Anatolian Sheepdogs into Britain also brought with them the massive spiked iron collars which such dogs still wear in Turkey.

Regrettably there is another type of spiked collar, with the spikes on the inside. This was used as a dog training device, particularly for the training of police and guard dogs on the Continent.

As well as wearing spiked collars for protection, dogs wore them for the offensive against their master's enemies. Many tribes, but notably the Gauls and the Huns, took dogs into battle with them. The description of these dogs shows that they were armoured, though no such early suit of dog armour has come down to us. The armour was covered with both spikes and knives, and a dog wearing it could be expected to cause havoc among both infantry and cavalry. Later dog armour was produced to protect boarhounds from the slashing attacks of the boar's tusks. This armour could consist of a set of splinter plates which were strapped round the dog, or a suit of chain mail with a high collar protecting the neck. Boarhounds also wore quilted or canvas coats. The latter were made of several layers of canvas stitched together. The stitching gave additional stiffness, and eyelet holes were left for ventilation.

Naturally, when dogs were so highly prized, the kennels they were kept in were also pretty lavish. The royal kennels were on the Isle of Dogs in London and a succession of monarchs kept the finest hounds and mastiffs there. Hunting was a passion throughout Tudor and early Stuart times and to be Master of the Buckhounds was a privileged position carrying a large salary. Few early kennels have survived, probably because dogs were as destructive then as they are today. One stone kennel in England has had a preservation order put on it as being of historical importance. An indoor kennel built for Marie Antoinette's lapdogs was recently on show in London. It is made of gilded wood, and bears the royal stamp with her monogram. Lined with padded blue velvet it has a blue satin cushion on the floor. It would be tempting to think that this belonged to the little white dog who, after her death, refused food and comfort and died of a broken heart.

Dogs have also been given badges of rank. The Greyhounds who had the privilege of appearing at the court of the Emperor Charlemagne with their masters, had their right paw closely shaven as a mark to indicate that they were dogs to respect. Sporting dogs too had to have distinguishing marks. An account of bull-baiting in 1694 says 'I must tell you that the famed dogs have crosses or roses of various coloured ribbon stuck with pitch upon their foreheads; and such like the ladies are very ready to bestow on dogs that do valiantly...'. So, nowadays, coursing Greyhounds are distinguished by one wearing a red favour and the other a white about their necks. Trail hounds are marked on the muzzle with a coloured crayon before each race.

Man has not hesitated either to chop off the pieces of the dog that he has felt to be superfluous. At one stage, the passion for hunting was so great that laws were passed to mutilate all dogs living near the king's preserves, so that they would be incapable of disturbing the game. The first of these forest laws was passed in the time of Canute, and stated that all dogs living within ten miles of a royal forest had to be hamstrung. The only exceptions were dogs small enough to pass through a dog gauge, that is an oval ring about seven inches by five in diameter. Laws of this kind remained in force for many centuries, though 'knee cutting' gave way to 'lawing' where three toes of the dog's forefoot were cut off with a blow from a chisel. Those found in the possession of unlawed dogs had to pay a fine.

Breeds of dog that are required to have layback or receding noses have also been subject to manipulation in the past. It is said that the eunuchs in charge of the Lion Dogs of the Peking Palaces would sit for many hours firmly pressing in the noses of young puppies in order to get them to recede. Mr. Edward C. Ash describes how Bulldogs were dealt with in the mid-nineteenth century. 'When the puppies were quite young and the muscles and bones of the face yet tender, the cords on the middle and two sides of the lips were cut. A small wooden block, hollowed out

A young Great Dane with cropped ears. Ear cropping was banned in Britain by the Kennel Club in 1895.

61

Someone always calls when
I've got my curlers in

A street beauty parlour
for Poodles in France

to fit the face, was then attached, and struck a sharp blow with a mallet. This drove back the cartilage and bone of the nose. Jacks were then attached to hold the face in its new position until the bones and muscles had set.'

Cosmetic surgery still goes on. One of the congenital defects fairly common in dogs, though present in many other species of animal, is entropion. This is an abnormality where the eyelids turn inwards causing acute irritation of the eye. This can be corrected surgically quite easily. Unfortunately dogs so treated are still often bred from, thus spreading the defect even more widely. The American Kennel Club does ban dogs with entropion from the show ring, but the operation to relieve the condition makes it virtually undetectable.

The cropping of dogs' ears was banned in Britain by the Kennel Club in 1895. The custom arose because in dog fighting and kindred sports a large ear provided a good hold for the dog's opponent. The Turks cut off the ears of their sheepdogs and fed them back to them in the belief that this would make the dogs stronger and fiercer.

Tail docking is a custom which is still practised. There do not seem to be many very valid reasons for the removal of something which the dog uses as a signal and as an aid to balance. However, breeders of the dogs whose tails are normally shortened would look askance at any suggestion that the practice should cease. The eye gets so accustomed to fashion that a Cocker Spaniel with a tail would appear a monstrosity.

Many dogs are of course, trimmed or clipped to conform to the prevailing fashion. In some terrier breeds, trimming has become a fine art, occupying many hours of the owner's time. The length and amount of hair left on a dog can help to disguise faults of conformation underneath. Poodles can be clipped in a variety of styles, though in Britain adults are invariably shown in the Lion clip. There are two theories as to how this particular fancy design originated. Early Poodles were used by wildfowlers as water dogs, and the hair on the hindquarters was clipped so that it should not impede the dog too much in the water. The bracelets were left on the legs to protect the joints from the cold. Another theory is that the clip is based on the court dress of the Louis XIV period. The hair left on in the Lion clip represents the full-bottomed wig, cape and knee breeches of the period, with ruffles round the wrists, knees and ankles. As with trimming, the art in clipping is to emphasise the dog's virtues while minimising the faults. Toy dogs also get their share of hairdressing. Though the Yorkshire Terrier with its coat oiled and protected by paper curlers may look rather ridiculous, most dogs enjoy the fuss and human attention they get while being groomed.

A considerable industry is now devoted to the modern dog's cosmetic needs. Electric clippers and driers, hair lotions and shampoos are produced to help the beautifying process. The dog can be dyed to match the owner's spring outfit and have its toenails painted gold or silver. Show dogs have their teeth cleaned and scaled, and a guard dog was recently fitted with false teeth so that it could continue on the job. The Americans have produced a dog cookery book, while in London you can dial for a dog's dinner to be delivered to the door. Doggie bags are advertised, so that owners dining out can get their money's worth by taking home the scraps. The desire to dress the dog up is also catered for. Pants to protect the bitch in season from unwanted attentions are on the market. They are made in a number of sizes and colours, but tartan and lurex models cost extra. Fashion shows are held to demonstrate swimsuits and rainwear, motoring goggles and bootees, and pyjamas for the dog to wear while lying on its superfoam, pneumatic dog bed. Clean, hygenic, indestructible dog toys include a simulated lamb chop of cow hide and a rather unbending slipper of the same material. A rubber bone can be bought for six times the price of a real one. Finally for those dogs that are still unhappy about modern life, pet tranquillisers can be bought to help them adjust.

Rear view of the Continental clip

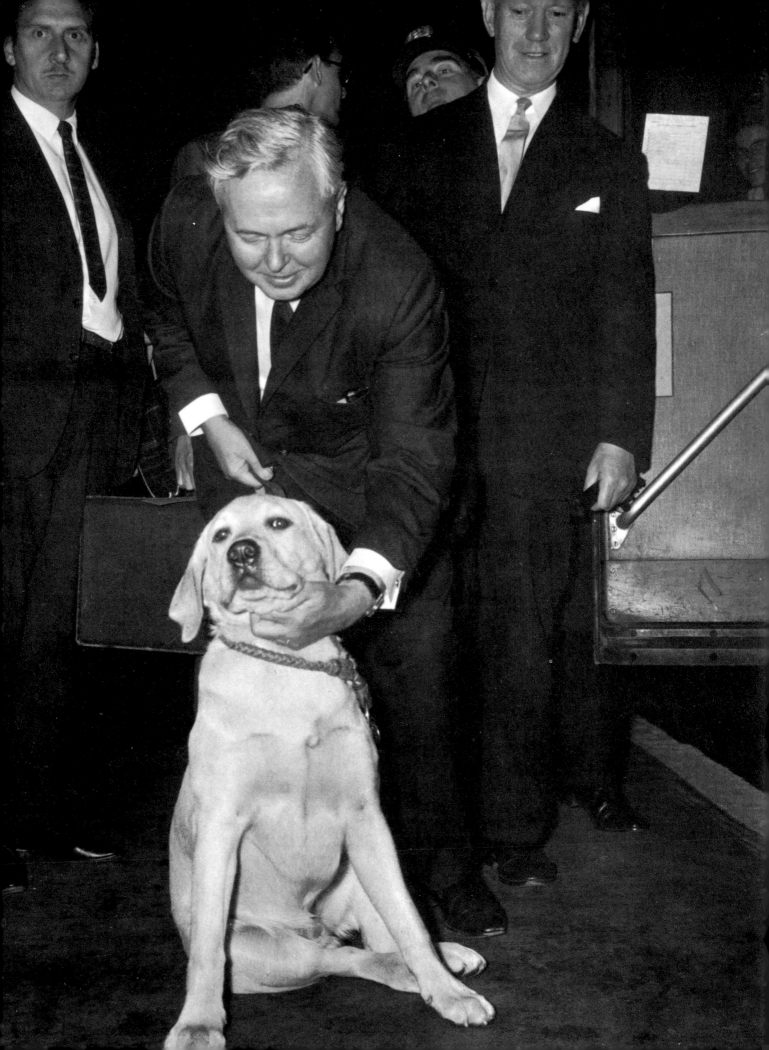

FAMOUS PEOPLE
AND THEIR DOGS

Princess Margaret and Lord
Snowdon leading a Labrador and a
Cavalier King Charles Spaniel

Mr Harold Wilson with his yellow Labrador Retriever

The King Charles Spaniel was named after Charles II, shown in this picture as a Prince with his brother and sisters.
The Spaniel is overshadowed here by the enormous Mastiff.

Elizabeth Taylor and her husband, Richard Burton, during a visit to London kept their dogs in a boat moored on the Thames in order to avoid putting them in quarantine

Pop group leader Dave Clark with his Great Dane

Glamorous film star of the 1930s, Jean Harlow, accompanied by her equally elegant Borzoi

Actress Jane Fonda photographed
with her two Whippets

Here is a dog famous in its
own right, Laika,
the Russian space dog

Corgis are the firm favourites of the Queen and the Royal Family

TO A BLACK GREYHOUND

Shining black in the shining light,
Inky black in the golden sun,
Graceful as the swallow's flight,
Light as swallow, winged one,
Swift as driven hurricane—
Double-sinewed stretch and spring,
Muffled thud of flying feet,
See the black dog galloping,
Hear his wild foot-beat.

See him lie when day is dead,
Black curves curled on the boarded floor.
Sleepy eyes, my sleepy-head —
Eyes that were aflame before.
Gentle now, they burn no more;
Gentle now and softly warm,
With the fire that made them bright
Hidden — as when after storm
Softly falls the night.

JULIAN GRENFELL

Greyhound racing at White
City Stadium in London

HOUNDS

The hound group contains two entirely different kinds of hunting dogs. The 'gazehounds' follow their quarry by sight and capture it by using great speed. They include such breeds as the Greyhound, Deerhound, Irish Wolfhound, Afghan Hound and Saluki. These coursing hounds have a very ancient history in the Middle East where, in the clear desert air, a Saluki will sight a bird in flight half a mile away.

The second group of hounds are those that hunt by scent. These too probably came from the Middle East; but when they reached the cooler, moist, heavily vegetated lands further north, they were bred with a greater diversity of type and greater scenting ability. A temperate climate affords better scenting conditions than a Mediterranean one, and it is therefore not suprising that Europe was the cradle of the greatest number of hound breeds.

All hounds that hunt by scent have certain characteristics in common. They are nearly all short-coated dogs with pendulous ears and plenty of stamina and perseverance. They are slower than the coursing hounds, being bred to wear down their quarry by their endurance in following a trail rather than to overcome it by superior speed. Coursing hounds run mute, needing all their breath for their physical exertion. Hounds bred to follow a scent give tongue while doing so. This enables the huntsman to know where they are, and to gauge from the quality of their cry how hot the line is that they are following, and whether they have their prey at bay. Most hounds, having been bred for centuries to live in packs, are not particularly aggressive towards other dogs, but they are both independent and stubborn. These are invaluable qualities when hunting a cold line, but not always desirable in a pet.

All dogs depend much more on scent and hearing than does man. Not only can a dog detect an odour in minute concentrations, it can also determine the direction from which the smell is coming. This is because the dog's nasal cavity is divided almost completely by bone, giving in effect two noses which gauge the direction of smell in much the same way as two eyes gauge the distance of an object and two ears gauge the direction of a sound. The enormous olfactory membrane is wrinkled and convoluted. It is estimated that were it stretched out flat it would equal in size the skin of the dog.

A number of factors go to make up a scent. A hunted animal will have its own particular odour, much increased by physical exertion. This may be picked up by a dog with its head up as a wind-borne scent, or it may

Champion Afghan Hound, Shere of Jarjih

73

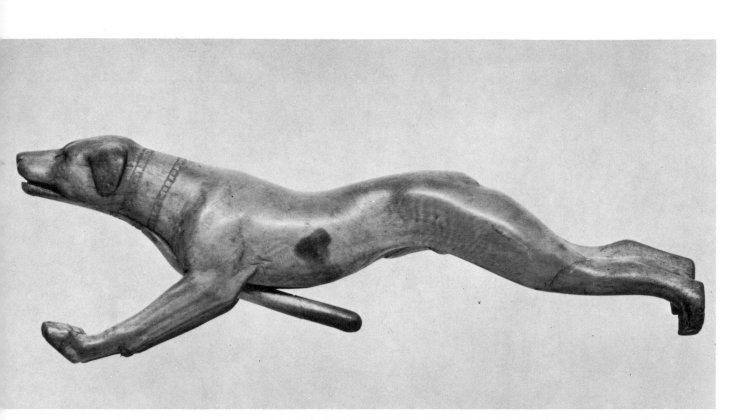

An ancient Egyptian toy in the form of a hound in full cry. Its lower jaw moves when the rod is manipulated.

The Beagle is popular as a pet in both Britain and the United States

be followed by a hound as a ground scent, in which case it will be mixed with the smell of bruised vegetation, crushed insects etc. The scent of a man will consist not only of his personal odour, which depends to some extent on how clean he is, but also of his footwear, clothing and of where he has recently been.

All scent evaporates and so a trail is obviously greatly affected by climatic conditions. The factors affecting scent are almost as complex as meteorology itself, but a mild, dull, humid day is most favourable. Scent lies longest where the ground temperature is higher than the air temperature, therefore tracking is easier at night. Overshadowed going, or soft, moist ground also help. A hot sun, strong wind, very heavy rain or a ground fouled by people, vehicles or strong-smelling substances all make scenting difficult. In general a scent more than twenty-four hours old can only be followed in exceptional circumstances by exceptional breeds such as Bloodhounds.

Bloodhounds have always been famed for their ability to follow a cold line. They are believed to have been introduced into Britain soon after the Norman Conquest. Their forerunner, the St. Hubert Hound, was bred at St. Hubert's Abbey in the Ardennes from the eighth century onwards. The St. Hubert Hound was either all white, or all black, and it is from the latter that the modern Bloodhound is descended. The Normans introduced the Bloodhound for hunting game but it was soon also used for tracking criminals. It was used on the borders of England and Scotland to track the Border raiders, and later in history to track those who poached game or stole sheep. Bloodhounds are seldom used today by the British police because they cannot be trained either to attack, or to hold their quarry once they have found him. In Britain a dual purpose dog like the Alsatian is preferred for police work, as these can be trained both to track a criminal and to hold him once they have found him. In America Bloodhounds are employed widely and successfully by the police of various States. There are many stories of almost incredible feats of tracking. Three Californian Bloodhounds led their handlers to the body of a boy who had been missing for 337 hours, and tracks of over fifty miles are not considered remarkable.

The black St. Hubert was also one of the progenitors of the Cuban

This Basset Hound is falling
over backwards to please

Beagles are used to hunt
the hare and are followed on foot

One of Hercules' tasks was to capture the three-headed spirit dog, Cerberus

A variety of dogs used for stag hunting appear in this painting by Pisanello

Bloodhound. This breed is now probably extinct but was developed specifically to hunt runaway slaves on the sugar plantations of the West Indies. This sort of Bloodhound crossed with Foxhound helped to create the American Coonhounds. This group of hounds includes the Bluetick Coonhound, the Redbone Hound, the Treeing Walker Hound and the Black and Tan Coonhound. Only the latter is recognised by the American Kennel Club, but all are specialists in raccoon hunting which is a widespread and popular sport. The hounds are required to pick up the trail, force the raccoon to take sanctuary in a tree and remain baying at it until the hunter can arrive with his gun.

The most widespread hound in Britain is of course the Foxhound. This hound probably owes something to the white St. Hubert. Ancestors of the Talbot family came from the Ardennes and settled in England in the eleventh century; they brought with them white hounds which became known as Talbots, and which were popular in the Middle Ages. These hounds were extinct by the end of the seventeenth century, and are now commemorated only on a few pub signs. They gave rise to the Southern Hound which was a slow, heavily built animal with an excellent nose. This hound was crossed with other dogs to give it more speed, and about 1700 the first recognisable Foxhounds appeared.

Centuries of selective breeding, where function was given greater importance than looks, have produced a beautiful hound, usually standing about twenty-four inches high, well boned, and with enormous stamina. When it is realised that Foxhounds may cover seventy miles on a hunting day, stamina is obviously essential. Type differs slightly with different packs, faster hounds being required for open country. Fell hounds are different again, being followed on foot or by binoculars over country

A medieval tapestry showing hounds used for bear hunting

A Talbot Hound depicted
on a pub sign in Oxfordshire

that no horseman could negotiate. Despite the increasing restrictions
on hunting imposed by urbanisation, there are now a greater number of
packs (more than 200) recognised in Britain by the Master of Foxhounds
Association, than there were before the Second World War. It is calcu-
lated that some five-sixths of the country is hunted over and that some
13,000 foxes are killed each year. Foxhounds have their own stud-books
and their own shows, the chief of which is the Peterborough Hound Show
held in July.

American Foxhounds are racier in build than the English Foxhound,
and greater diversity in their use has led to greater diversity of type. Some
seventeenth century colonists sailing to America took with them their
packs of hounds and these formed the basis for the American Foxhound.
There are four main uses for these very popular sporting dogs today.
Field trials are run in which speed and a competitive nature are essentials.
Some slow hounds are bred to hunt the fox and be followed on foot by a
man with a gun. Hunt Clubs and hunting farmers follow packs of hounds
as is done in England; and drag hounds are raced, following an arti-
ficially laid scent.

English Foxhounds
of the Eridge Hunt

The huntsman seems to be
in despair at his hounds'
disregard of the hare in this
etching by Hollar

Following a drag with Trail Hounds is becoming an increasingly popular sport in the north of Britain. Hound trails started at the beginning of this century with Foxhounds from the Fell packs. These were crossed with anything that would give them more speed while not detracting from the stamina they need to race across the screes and fells of the Lake District and Westmorland. Today's Trail Hounds are very racy in outline and they follow a trail of aniseed, turpentine and paraffin laid by a man walking the circular course and dragging an impregnated cloth behind him. Senior trails cover a ten mile course, and betting on the result probably accounts for the increasing popularity of the sport.

The Beagle is another hound breed with a very ancient history. Small hounds like this are believed to have been used in Britain since before the Roman invasion. Beagle packs nowadays hunt the hare, and are followed on foot by people whose main pleasure is derived from watching a hound hunt a line. The hare is a very cunning adversary and will leave a trail like a maze to confuse the hounds, so Beagles have to be painstaking in pursuit and not so fast that they outrun the human field.

The Afghan hunts by sight
and relies on speed and agility
to capture its quarry

The start of a hound trail in the north of England

There is grave danger of two kinds of Beagles being produced, as the
Beagle started to become very popular as a pet in Britain in the late
1950s. This trend occurred earlier in America and imports of the smaller
American hound were made into Britain. More Beagles are kept as
companions and for the show ring than are hunted in packs, and as their
hunting ability cannot be judged in the ring this quality will most probably deteriorate.

The Basset Hound is another that has recently become very popular
as a pet. These hounds also go back to the St. Hubert Hound, but though
so long known in France, the first pair did not reach Britain until 1866.
There are about ten packs of these hounds hunting the hare in Britain.
They are reputed to have the finest noses and the most melodious cry
of any of the hounds that are hunted in packs. Those used for their
original purpose are higher and straighter on the leg than the ones seen
in the show ring. Basset Hounds have a deceptively doleful appearance
and their short legs make people think of them as smaller than they are.
In fact Bassets are large, low-slung dogs that need a lot of food and
plenty of exercise.

There are also a number of packs of Harriers, Staghounds and Otterhounds in Britain. Harriers — small hounds bred to hunt hares — were
used by the ancient Greeks. The modern packs, which are followed by
a mounted field, consist of hounds eighteen inches or so high at the shoulder. Staghounds proper, such as were known in Elizabethan times, no
longer exist. The six or so hunts in Britain which hunt deer use large
Foxhounds for the purpose. Otterhound packs too use mainly Foxhounds.
The Otterhound itself is a breed which has nearly disappeared in Britain.
They are black, blue or red dogs with tan markings, and have wonderful

The Grosvenor Hunt by Stubbs, 1762

American Foxhounds at a meet in the U.S.A.

Otterhounds have a close, oily coat which can withstand long periods of immersion in water

Home, James!

noses. Their coats are harsh and wiry, with a woolly undercoat. One pure-bred pack still exists in Scotland. In America both the Harrier and the Otterhound are quite popular as show dogs.

Though few men now hunt for food, more and more do so for recreation. Hounds in all their different guises have never been more popular, and as long as man remains a hunter by nature their future seems assured.

The English Foxhound must have very strong and straight front legs

My hounds are bred out of the Spartan kind,
So flewed, so sanded; and their heads are hung
With ears that sweep away the morning dew;
Crook-kneed, and dew-lapped like Thessalian bulls,
Slow in pursuit, but matched in mouth like bells,
Each unto each. A cry more tunable
Was never hollaed to, nor cheered with horn,
In Crete, in Sparta, nor in Thessaly:
Judge when you hear.

WILLIAM SHAKESPEARE.
MIDSUMMER NIGHT'S DREAM. ACT IV, SCENE I.

Bassets used for hunting have
longer and straighter legs than
those bred for showing

The Basset Hound has recently become very popular as a pet

DRAUGHT DOGS

The use of dogs for haulage work was a very widespread and ancient practice that has almost vanished in modern times. Marco Polo mentions that he saw dogs used to draw sledges over mud and ice too slippery for horse or wheeled traffic. Throughout Mongolia, Tibet, Northern China and Manchuria, Mastiff-type dogs hauled loads over terrain unsuitable for hoofed animals. Europe and the Low Countries followed suit, though more often because the use of a dog rather than a horse was more economical for a small trader, than because going was too rough for the horse. The dogs that were used were again Mastiff-like animals, with broad heads, blunt muzzles and short to medium length coats. Further north, in countries bordering the Arctic circle, the Spitz type of dog was used exclusively. Pricked ears, pointed muzzle, bushy tail and dense coat are the common features of all the sledge dogs of the north.

In the Low Countries, particularly in Belgium, and also in Switzerland, dogs were commonly used during the nineteenth and early twentieth centuries to take farm produce to market. They delivered bread and milk, hauled coal and fish, and brought cheeses and wickerwork down from the Swiss Cantons. The size of dog, type of harness and weight of load were stipulated by law, and inspectors made spot checks on the dogs as they worked and on the licences of their owners. The dogs were usually harnessed between shafts, with the main strain of the weight behind them taken by a broad band across the chest. Sometimes the dog was harnessed by a single trace and the cart had a shaft at the back for the driver to hold. This enabled the dog to seek shade when the cart was at rest, and also to guard the load more effectively. Any dog that was big enough would be used for this type of work. In Switzerland, three of the four Swiss Mountain breeds are used for haulage — the Appenzell Mountain Dog, the Bernese Mountain Dog and the Great Swiss Mountain Dog. These are believed to be the descendants of the droving dogs brought over the Alps by the invading Roman armies.

The custom of using draught dogs spread from the Low Countries to Britain, though not very far north for they were unknown in Scotland. By the early nineteenth century dogs were pulling butchers', bakers' and milkmaids' carts. They were hauling builders' supplies, knife-grinding machines and tinkers' barrows. Costers took their families out in dog-drawn carts. A dog might pull a baby carriage, or a brace might be harnessed to a children's chaise. In the south of England dogs were used to take fish from the ports to the railheads. A team of four dogs could

This nineteenth century dog cart looks somewhat overloaded

Dogs were frequently used for light traffic in Holland and Belgium. These two pictures show a milk cart and a baker's van.

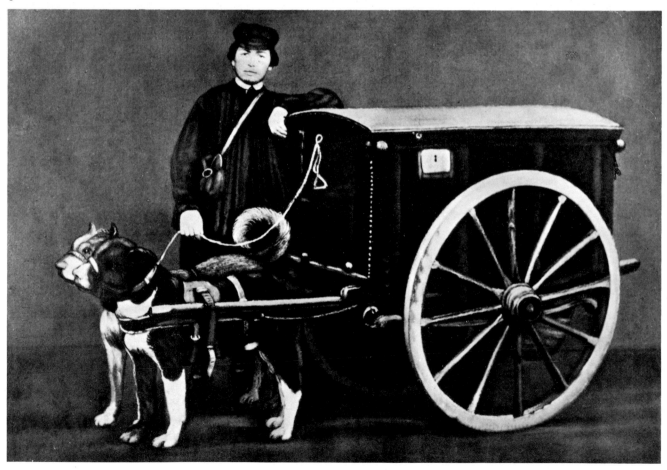

A dog-drawn bakery
cart in Bruges

Skiing the easy way with
the help of two St Bernards

pull three to four hundredweight and such teams are reported to have
gone from Brighton to Portsmouth in a day. In 1820 a Monsieur Chabert
arrived in London from Bath with 'a great Siberian wolf dog' (presumably
some sort of Husky). He boasted that his dog could pull him in his gig
for thirty miles a day. He did not win his wager for the dog only managed
twenty miles.

This Portugese Water Dog has
had his hindquarters clipped
in the traditional manner

The banning of draught dogs in England was not really for humanita-
rian reasons. They were disliked in London because they were alleged to
frighten the horses, and they made an abominable noise about their
work, particularly in the early morning. In 1839, the Metropolitan police
banned all draught dogs within a fifteen mile radius of Charing Cross.
This was a measure designed to reduce traffic chaos which was already
considerable, and it led to the destruction of some 3,000 dogs. In 1854,
the ban became general throughout England.

One of the most popular breeds in the early 1800s was the Newfoundland. They were often used in England as draught dogs but were more
widely employed still in Newfoundland itself. During the fishing season
the dogs hauled in the nets and took the catch from the boats to the drying
sheds. They were also used as pack animals, taking mail to the outlying

Newfoundlands were employed
for more serious draught jobs
than this in their native land

The name Husky is used
to describe any Spitz type of dog
used for sledge work. The team
in the top picture formed part
of Scott's Antarctic Expedition.
Those in the centre picture
are being used for seal hunting
in Canada's North
West Territories.

A dog team at Coppermine
in the North West Territories
of Canada

parts of the island. In winter teams of dogs hauled wood, and it is said that a single dog could earn enough to support its owner throughout the winter. Being powerful and hardy Newfoundlands have also been used for sledge work. They were used by the Americans in the Second World War for haulage work in Alaska. Their strength and dependability compared favourably with the breeds of Husky, but their feet were too tender for continual work on ice and the Newfoundlands had to be provided with rawhide bootees.

Newfoundlands were originally fishermens' dogs. In Europe the Portuguese Water Dog accompanied the Portuguese fishing fleet. This breed's history can be traced back to the fourteenth century, and they are believed to be closely related to the Poodle. The similarity between the two breeds is accentuated by the fact that the Portuguese Water Dog had its back, loins, hind-legs and tail clipped during the summer months. The dogs were powerful and enthusiastic swimmers, which were expected to retrieve anything that fell overboard, help haul the fishing nets, and carry messages from boat to boat and boat to shore. During the present century the need for such a dog declined and their numbers were much reduced. They are still however, bred and exhibited.

The sledge dogs of the north are also being superseded by mechanical transport, though it seems unlikely that the need for them will entirely disappear for some while. Without these dogs, living in the Arctic would have been impossible for the Eskimo tribes, and for the fur-traders and prospectors. Living conditions for the dogs were harsh and their treatment often brutal. Understandably, sledge dogs got a reputation for ferocity. If treated with consideration and kindness however, they have been proved to be no more unreliable than any other breed of dog. Obviously they need firm handling and a good deal of exercise, but increasing numbers of the various Husky breeds are being kept as pets on both sides of the Atlantic.

The word husky is a corruption of 'esky', a slang diminutive of 'Eskimo', and it is generally used to cover any Spitz type of dog used for sledge work. In the past there were a number of distinct types of Husky, but with the influx of Europeans northwards, much cross-breeding took place. During the Yukon gold rush in particular, any animal that was big enough was used to haul a sledge. Most teams consisted of mongrels, and a number of pure-bred Husky types disappeared completely.

Today there are four main breeds of sledge dog. These are the Samoyed, the Alaskan Malamute, the Greenland Dog and the Siberian Husky. Of these the Samoyed is recognised by the Kennel Clubs of America and Great Britain. These dogs have been pure-bred for a very long time and were originally the companions of a nomadic tribe who roamed the Siberian tundra. The dogs were used for herding reindeer, hunting and sledge work. They were highly valued by their owners and lived in the nomads' tents as part of the family. This close contact with the human race has produced a gentle, goodnatured dog which is highly adaptable. In its homeland the Samoyed could be found in all colours, but in Britain and America only white, cream or biscuit colouring is allowed. The dense, double coat is harsh with a stand-off ruff, and the average height is about twenty-one inches. The expression of the Samoyed is important. Due to a natural curve of the lips the dog always appears to be smiling.

The Malamutes were a tribe of Eskimos who lived on the Seward peninsula. They also valued their sledge dogs highly and bred them with care. When the Arctic was opened up by traders and missionaries the Malamute dogs became more widely known and were greatly esteemed. The gold rush era very nearly saw the extinction of the pure-bred Alaskan Malamute, but enough were left for the breed to be recognised by the American Kennel Club in 1926. Since then the Malamute has achieved a certain popularity as a companion and for sleigh racing. It stands up to twenty-five inches at the shoulder and is rather longer in the back than most other Huskies. Malamutes are usually wolf-grey or black and white, and often have markings on the head resembling either a cap or a mask.

The Siberian Husky is probably the smallest and the fastest of the sledge dog breeds. They were imported into Alaska in 1909 and soon made their name in sledge dog racing. They have a smooth-textured

Huskies taking part
in the British Trans-Arctic
Expedition of 1968

A pet Labrador provides
the motive power for an
unusual baby carriage

double coat which gives them a cleaner outline than the more heavily coated Husky breeds. They can be any colour and many have very striking blue eyes.

The Greenland Dog is also known as the Eskimo Dog and is the type most often seen in Great Britain, where they are rather confusingly known as Huskies. A wide range of size and colour is permissible. Two of these dogs went with Scott on his last Antarctic expedition, though the rest of his dog teams consisted of Siberian Huskies. They are not a recognised breed in Britain or America.

As well as for hauling sledges, the Eskimo used the Husky to hunt seal and polar bear. In the summer the dogs were occasionally used as pack animals, carrying a load of twenty pounds or so in panniers on their backs. When harnessed as a sledge team, the dogs are usually fastened in pairs to a central trace, the leader being on his own out in front. The fan hitch is slowly going out of favour. Here the dogs are fastened to the sledge each with his own trace, so that they fan out ahead of the sledge when pulling. This is impractical over wooded or very rough country. A third method has a single file of dogs hitched between two traces. The harness is usually canvas or webbing, though it used to be leather. Huskies have been known to vary their monotonous and scanty diet by eating the harness and the boots of their driver when they could get hold of them. Eskimo sledges tended to be built of whatever was at hand and were often rather heavy. A dog team will average four miles an hour, though

94

A handsome Husky in Canada. The team on the left was used on Scott's Antarctic expedition in 1911.

of course much higher speeds can be achieved when necessary. Some incredible journeys with sledge dogs have been recorded. One of the most famous was that of a team carrying medical supplies which covered a distance of 522 miles from Winnipeg to St. Paul in the remarkable time of four days, twenty-two hours.

Sledge dog racing is an increasingly popular sport in North America. The best known race is the Alaskan Dog Derby held over a 412 mile course. Siberian Huskies are most commonly used, and the record for the race stood for many years at eighty hours, twenty-seven minutes. Much shorter races are also held, though the dogs used for these are often Huskies crossed with Alsatians or Collies to give them more speed. A lightweight, forty pound sledge is used. The number of dogs in a team is not specified but seven is usual, as more tend to slow the pace. Quebec has a circular thirty-three mile course which has been covered in one hour, fifty minutes.

INSCRIPTION ON THE TOMB AT NEWSTEAD ABBEY OF BOATSWAIN, A NEWFOUNDLAND

"Near this spot
Are deposited the Remains of one
Who possessed Beauty without Vanity,
Strength without Insolence,
Courage without Ferocity,
And all the Virtues of Man without his Vices.
This Praise, which would be unmeaning Flattery
If inscribed over human ashes,
Is but a just tribute to the Memory of
BOATSWAIN, a Dog,
Who was born at Newfoundland, May, 1803,
And died at Newstead Abbey, Nov. 18, 1808."

GUARD DOGS

Wild dogs are prepared to defend the territory they inhabit against intruders. This instinct to protect an area and warn off intruders could have been the first contact between man and dog. Primitive man, having attracted a pack of wild dogs to scavenge round his camp, would have received prior warning of the approach of other tribesmen or of large carnivores by watching the behaviour of the dogs.

Certainly guard dogs have been in the service of man for as long as recorded history, and they are also woven into the mythology of many peoples. The spirit dogs, such as Cerberus guarding the gates of Hades, are found in legends all over the world. They are described as terrible in aspect and invincible in strength. Obviously early guard dogs, which had to protect the flocks from wolves, as well as their master's property from thieves, were animals which prudent strangers avoided. The watchdogs that guarded the halls of the Vikings, were turned loose each night to roam the camp. When evening came, strangers and guests were formally introduced to the dogs before the animals were loosed. Any man who at this meeting was regarded suspiciously by the dogs, was apt to find himself cold-shouldered by his hosts as well.

The Romans left a number of descriptions of their guard dogs, which were Mastiff-like in type. Used at home as protection against thieves, dogs like these also went to war with the Roman legionaries, guarding the camps and provisions against marauders. In Britain the Mastiff has been known since the earliest times, and the word itself may be a corruption of 'master of thief'. Watchdogs were often known as bandogs, meaning one that was tied up with a band or leash. Any dog that spends a large part of its life tied up becomes increasingly aggressive and suspicious. Indeed, keeping a watchdog perpetually chained was liable to defeat its purpose, as the animal had no chance to develop its intelligence or discrimination and would attack all and sundry. As a Roman writer said 'A watchdog should be neither too gentle nor too fierce, for if it is gentle it fawns on everyone including thieves, while if too fierce it will attack members of the household it defends.' A seventeenth century description of the perfect guard dog runs as follows: 'for this purpose you must provide you such a one, as hath a large and mightie body, a great and a shrill voyce, that both with his barking he may discover, and with his sight dismay the Theefe, yea, being not scene, with the horror of his voice put him to flight... his disposition must neither be too gentle, nor too curst, that he neither fawne upon a theefe, nor lavish of his

A mosaic 'beware of the dog' warning found at Pompeii

97

This drawing made in 1754
shows the type of unfortunate
guard dog that spent its days
tightly roped to a post

Hercules capturing
the three-headed Cerberus

mouth, barking without cause, neither maketh it any matter though he
be not swift: for he is but to fight at home, and to give warning of the
enemie.'

Nowadays guard dogs are being used more widely than ever but the
methods of employing them have changed radically. It is recognised that
an enormous, ferocious brute, perpetually chained, is not nearly so useful
as an alert, incorruptible dog that has been trained to obey orders and
is also intelligent enough to act on its own initiative. The guard dog
today is being put to increasingly sophisticated use and its training is
both complex and thorough.

It was the realisation, particularly during the Second World War, that
trained dogs with the services would do much to relieve the manpower
shortage, that gave the impetus to the increasingly wide use of dogs by
security firms. The guarding of airfields and ammunition dumps against
saboteurs was very wasteful of manpower. The R.A.F. in particular set
up a Police Dog Training School, and dogs and their handlers began to
patrol the perimeters of airfields and other R.A.F. establishments. A
well trained dog will scent an intruder 150 yards away, and will find and
keep the suspect from leaving until the handler arrives on the scene. These
dogs are not trained to attack unless ordered to do so or unless their
handler himself is attacked. Instead, on finding a criminal they will
circle him, barking continuously. Only if the suspect produces a weapon
will they attack the man's arm, attempting to swing him round and get
him off balance. The dog will do the same thing if the criminal attempts
to escape from custody or if the handler is attacked. This man work is
also an integral part of police dog training, and is definitely not the sort
of thing to be attempted by amateurs. A dog trained for man work is
potentially a lethal weapon, and a lot of security training is devoted to
seeing that the dog is under the complete control of its handler at all
times, and that every dog will leave the attack when ordered to do so.

The largest security firm in Britain employs over 700 dogs for guard

This police dog demonstrates a new idea for capturing fugitives from the air

Mobile police dog on patrol!

work, and there are probably several thousand in civilian employment in the country. These dogs usually start training between the ages of eight and eighteen months. Many of them, as with police and R.A.F. dogs, are given by members of the public, who have found that the lovable bundles of fluff that they bought at eight weeks have grown larger and more energetic than they had envisaged. Basically these dogs are taught to protect people carrying valuables, or to patrol and protect property. They are especially effective against pilfering, from building sites or parcels lorries for example. Whereas police dogs work with one handler only, commercial firms have found that they can train a dog to obey two or three. This means that when a man is ill or on holiday, his dog is still of use.

New uses for guard dogs are being found all the time. Dogs patrolling fuel stores can be taught to hold anyone producing matches or a lighter. Some police forces abroad have been experimenting with remote control. The dogs are sent out with a small radio receiver strapped to their backs, through which their handler transmits his orders.

Many breeds can be trained for guard work, though Alsatians are the breed most widely used. Many Alsatians when adult are naturally aloof with strangers and are both intelligent and incorruptible. The Dobermann Pinscher was developed in Germany at the end of the last century specifically for guard work, and is widely used on the Continent and in America. The Airedale Terrier, the Boxer and the Giant Schnauzer are also used by European police forces. In this country the Bullmastiff seems to have been unaccountably neglected. This breed was created by crossing the rather unwieldy Mastiff with the agile Bulldog prototype. This cross was tried in the nineteenth century by gamekeepers who wanted a dog active and powerful enough to catch and hold on to poachers. Bullmastiffs still make faithful companions and guards, but do not seem to have been used by any official body. The latest recruit to the breeds used by the police is the Rottweiler. These dogs were used as cattle drovers for

A demonstration showing how a trained dog will seize a man by the arm and attempt to throw him off balance

many centuries in southern Germany. Their numbers had declined very much by 1900, but realisation that they made good police dogs led to a breed renaissance. Several are now in training or on the beat in Britain.

As it is a fact that households with a dog are less likely to be broken into than those without, it is obviously desirable to encourage the family pet to give warning of intruders. It is often said of a dog that barks at the sound of the front door bell, that it is a good house-dog. This is not really true, for the animal which indicates something of which the owner is unaware is far more valuable. Small dogs with a loud bark can be just as effective in warning off intruders as large animals whose appearance alone will act as a deterrent. Most dogs have a latent protective instinct which may not develop until they are adult but which can be fostered by training. Puppies can be encouraged to growl or bark at unfamiliar sounds and to be silent otherwise. A dog that barks continually is an irritant that is finally ignored by everyone. If the dog is taught to discriminate between the familiar and the unfamiliar, then every warning sound the animal makes should be investigated, for a dog's hearing is more acute than a man's. It is valuable to teach a dog to refuse food offered by strangers and to leave alone any food found lying on the ground. Not only is this better for the dog's health in general, but it is not unknown for poisoned bait to be pushed through the letter box to silence a guard dog. When out for a walk in a lonely area, the dog should always be recalled by the owner when a stranger appears on the scene. Being put on the lead or made to walk at heel when someone unknown

This Alsatian attached to a security firm was called in to guard a farm in Kent against thieves and vandals

This chained-up dog was found in a farm out-building. The owner was convicted of causing it unnecessary suffering.

Police dog going over an assault course as part of its rigorous training

appears tends to make the dog more alert and suspicious. It is also a good idea to teach the dog to sit and stay in one place. Once this is learnt the dog can be left quietly in the hall each time the front door is opened. If a stranger is on the doorstep, the dog should remain where it is until he or she has gone. If friends of the family are there then the dog should be released from its position and allowed to greet them. Some dogs resent anyone entering their domain, so any signs of aggression towards friends of the family should be very firmly checked at the beginning, if necessary by sending the dog to its bed and keeping it there. If a dog is left to guard the contents of a car, a certain amount of forethought is necessary before the vehicle is parked. A dog left in a car that is parked in the sun, or parked where the sun will reach it before the owner's return, can suffer from heat-stroke.

Finally anyone who owns a dog at all should carry third party insurance. Dogs can cause accidents for which their owners are liable. Guard dogs should always be under control, but the very nature of their work suggests that insurance should be carried as an extra safeguard.

ODD JOBS

When Noah entered the Ark he took with him two dogs which according to legend were Afghan Hounds. Another story goes on to tell how the Ark sprang a leak which the dogs plugged with their noses. This explains why a dog's nose is always cold and wet! Ever since, man in his ingenuity has employed the dog in any number of curious ways.

Primitive man in many parts of the world used the dog in magical rites. The belief was widely held that dogs were guides to the spirit world and messengers to the gods. When a man died, some Red Indian tribes sacrificed a dog to guide him safely on his journey to the other world. Dogs have been sacrificed to exorcise evil spirits, to cure illnesses, to purify places and people, and to placate the gods. Dogs have been worshipped and ritually eaten by their worshippers.

The belief that direct contact with a dog would cure certain illnesses was a particularly widespread and long lasting one. In England during the fifteenth, sixteenth and seventeenth centuries small lapdogs were carried and were regarded as being very efficacious in relieving abdominal pains. These animals were often toy spaniels and were known as 'comforters'. They were also believed to attract their owner's fleas, and it may well be the case that these parasites did prefer the higher temperature of the dog. Many people have appreciated the constant warmth provided by a small dog. The Aztec priests of Mexico used 'pillow dogs' as hot water bottles. It is not known what kind of dogs these were. Some experts believe them to have been ancestors of the Chihuahua, while others consider them to have been a hairless variety. Tibetan lamas used dogs as foot warmers and also carried them in the sleeves of their gowns. Even today Australian Aborigines use Dingo pups, carried across the hip or shoulder, to provide warmth on cold desert mornings.

Dogs have also provided motive power for wheels. They have turned Buddhist prayer wheels in the Far East and water wheels in Scotland, churned butter in Wales, and turned roasting spits all over Europe. Any short-legged, smooth-coated dog would be used as a turnspit. Pictures of them show a variation in type from those resembling Dachshunds to those resembling Cardigan Corgis and small terriers. One variety, sufficiently distinct to be described by a contemporary as a 'turnspit tyke', had short bandy legs with a long body and a large head. The colour was bluish grey spotted with black, and the tail curled over the back. Queen Victoria kept two turnspits as pets at Windsor, but since then they have died out completely.

An Alsatian trained for film work walks the tightrope

Tipsy is so keen on retrieving darts at his local that he often has to be held until they have all been thrown

Rex finds it safer to gather up the empties

Mothering an orphaned piglet is certainly an odd job for this Boxer bitch

Dogs have been bred for fighting for a very long time and in many countries. The Mastiff, Bulldog, Bull Terrier, and Staffordshire Bull Terrier are all breeds whose origins are closely connected with wild animal baiting, bull baiting and organised dog fighting. Though organised dog fights have been banned by law nearly everywhere in the world, the fighting breeds survive, making in many cases excellent guard dogs. The Hong Kong Kennel Club recognise the Chinese Fighting Dog, a breed unknown in the West. This has been described as a dark, loose-skinned dog with curved canine teeth and a head resembling a hippopotamus. Dog fighting has been very popular in Japan too. At one time it was almost a cult. The Tosa or Japanese Mastiff has been known for at least six centuries, though it is a cross-bred type rather than a pure breed. Winning dogs were treated with the greatest honour.

In Europe, dogs have been used as lures for wildfowl for a number of centuries. Ducks and geese swimming on water display a great deal of curiosity about the movements of predators such as foxes on the banks. A dog, fox-like in build, was trained to lure the curious wildfowl into nets. Quite elaborate traps were constructed with netted tunnels leading from a central pond. The dogs were trained to run along the banks, appearing briefly in the gaps left in the concealing vegetation, to tempt the ducks and geese further inside the nets. The method has been used in Britain at the Wildfowl Trust in order to net birds for ringing. It is also used in America to lure ducks within the range of sportmens' guns.

It is more usual of course, for dogs to be used as bird scarers rather than bird lures. They have been used to clear airport runways of birds, and at Liverpool airport the amplified bark of a dog is played over the loudspeakers to clear the airfield of stray dogs. The Great Western Railway used to employ dogs on certain lines in Wales. The animals worked on their own, clearing the railway lines of stray sheep. The dog was expected to round these up and herd them back through any gap in the fencing that it might discover. They were also used to warn gangers working on the line of the approach of trains. They were trained not to leave the rails until everyone else was clear.

The scenting power of the dog has also been put to profitable use. Truffle hunting dogs are still used in Italy and were once widely used all

Others perform
tricks for a living

Some dogs just like to show off!

over the Continent. The last truffle hunter in Britain ceased work in the 1930s but in the eighteenth and nineteenth centuries fair numbers of trained dogs were in use all over southern England. Truffles are underground fungi which have always fetched a high price on the luxury food market. Dogs were rewarded with a titbit when they had indicated where digging would uncover a truffle. A school for training truffle dogs existed in Piedmont where a November truffle fair is also held. The Collins family were the most famous truffle hunters in England and they used small, white, curly-coated dogs which were believed to have come originally from France. This type of dog now seems to have become extinct and small cross-bred terriers now do the job on the Continent.

One of the famous Collins family digging for truffles near Salisbury with his Truffle Hounds in 1910

The Russians have recently trained dogs as geological prospectors. Ore deposits have characteristic smells, and their most highly trained

What more appropriate mascot for the 1st Battalion Irish Guards than an Irish Wolfhound?

At the Royal Aircraft Establishment, Farnborough, Rusty is specially trained to locate vital parts of crashed aircraft

This Sheepdog rounds up an unusual flock

A variety of breeds are trained as guide dogs for the blind

dog can detect one up to a depth of twenty-three feet.

The British police have also been training dogs to help find drugs. An Alsatian and a Labrador were chosen in the first place and trained to detect the drug cannabis. The dogs became so expert at this that they could detect drugs even in sealed containers. One Labrador, Pytch, has a number of arrests to his credit. Customs officials along the European land frontiers also use dogs to combat drug trafficking.

Trained Sheepdogs
are extremely lively
and intelligent

A Sheepdog in control
of a flock in Wiltshire

Glen, a football crazy Collie

Not all dogs are on the side of the law however. Smugglers themselves have used dogs to help them. The most famous of these was a Poodle called Barbou who was used to smuggle Belgian lace into France. The dog was clipped and the lace wound round his body. A fake coat of Poodle hair was then tied over him. The dog was taught to avoid anyone wearing a customs official's uniform. The colour of the faked coat was frequently changed to help hide the dog's identity but eventually the dog was shot while swimming a river.

Ever since the days when Romulus and Remus were suckled by a wolf, bitches have been used as foster mothers for the most unlikely orphan animals. The ideal bitch for a foster mother needs a strong maternal instinct and a placid nature. Sheepdogs very often seem to be given the role, and make newspaper headlines by rearing lion or tiger cubs in zoos. The maternal instinct of some bitches is so strong that they will produce milk for orphans placed in their care, whether they have recently had a litter themselves or not, and there are records of them rearing the most unlikely animals, including rabbits! There is another side to the picture. Travellers in Italy in the eighteenth century were shocked to see women suckling the pups of highly prized and delicate lapdogs. Eskimo women have also been known to rear orphaned Huskies with their own children, for survival in the Arctic depended on the sledge dog.

Finally perhaps we should take into account the immense debt that man owes the dog in medical research. A large number of dogs have lived and died helping man to find the cause and the means or preventing diabetes, human pellagra and rickets. The first blood transfusions and the first open heart operations were tried on dogs, and they were the first animals used to test the effect of radioactive substances. This list is neither exhaustive nor representative but it does serve to indicate the immense debt mankind owes to the dog.

The soft mouth of the Labrador and the Springer Spaniel make them ideal retrievers

This high speed Great Dane
earns large sums of money
in films and television

A trained Alsatian jumps
through a hoop of fire

DOGS IN ADVERTISING

The silhouette inn sign
of 'The Black Dog'
near Salisbury, Wilts

Registered trademark of the
Gramophone Company Limited.
This painting by
Francis Barraud has been
reproduced more times than any
other picture, and has become
the most famous trademark
in the world.

The Two Dogs — a Scottish
Terrier and a West Highland
White — have become famous
as the trademark of
'Black & White' Scotch Whisky

Cruft's Dog Show is traditionally advertised by the use
of this poster with its picture of a St Bernard

Symbol of Britain, the Bulldog
is used on this poster
to encourage people to invest
in National Savings

Kennels in Essex called
'Ye Spotted Dog Inn'

your National Savings

put power into
the pound

The unique old inn sign of the 'Fox and Hounds' at Barley, Herts. It shows fox,
hounds, huntsman and whipper-in, racing along the top of the beam.

That's a comfortable pair of shoes you've got there, you lucky dog!

This famous advertisement for Spratts dog biscuits has been in use for many years

Hush Puppies are a girl's best friend. Because Hush Puppies aren't just comfortable. They resist mud, scuffs, stains, dirt. Brush clean in seconds. Light, flexible Hush Puppies are made of breathing brushed pigskin. And they stay comfortable right to the end of the road. CECILE 79/11

Hush Puppies®
BRAND

IN BREATHING BRUSHED PIGSKIN

Everywhere — for men, women and children

A mournful Basset Hound appears on every advertisement for 'Hush Puppies' shoes. The choice of this breed reflects its fast growing popularity with the public

This novel sign shows a mug painted with two hounds, the fox forming its handle

The fine carved signboard over the doorway of the 'Cat and Fiddle' at Hinton Admiral, Hampshire. This name was derived from 'Catherine Fidelis' which was the old title of the inn.

JOHN SIDNEY MAFFEY. LICENSED TO RETAIL WINES, SPIRITS, BEER & TOBACCO.

The Old English Sheepdog lends appeal to advertisements for Dulux paint

PUPPIES

Puppies are irresistible, so any clear thinking about buying one should be done before looking at them. A well chosen dog as a family pet can repay a thousandfold the trouble and responsibility of keeping it, but acquiring a puppy is akin to adding a new member to the family, and a little thought beforehand can save a great deal of irritation later. The person who will look after the dog should be the one to decide how much money he or she can afford to spend on feeding it and how much time on exercising and grooming it. If a particular breed appeals more than any other, try to consider the disadvantages as well as the pleasures of ownership. Some people even seem surprised that their tiny puppy should grow up into a large dog, so some other foreseeable hazards should perhaps be listed. Some small dogs are noisy, and some so energetic that they are rarely still. A breed with hairy legs and feet will bring in a bucketful of mud at each outing and a large dog will empty all the ashtrays every time it wags its tail. Whether these considerations are major or minor ones rather depends on the temperament of the owner, but they are all worth thinking about beforehand.

Though all dog owners will argue the merits of their relative pets unceasingly, all will agree that picking a healthy puppy is the first essential. Puppies are either living life to the full or are sound asleep, so the listless, disinterested one should be avoided. Temperamental differences show at a very early age so the puppy that hangs back or is easily startled in familiar surroundings will certainly be nervous in strange ones. Healthy puppies are clean and plump with loose supple skin and clear eyes. Discharging eyes or nose, or evidence of diarrhoea, should be cause for suspicion. If the parents of the pups can be seen, their behaviour will give some clues as to the likely character of their offspring. Check to see that your prospective purchase has had the dewclaws removed from the hindlegs, and that it has not got an umbilical hernia. Both these could cause trouble later on. If the litter seems healthy and well-fed, then the old adage about picking the largest and the boldest of the puppies is not a bad one to follow.

Finding a puppy of the kind you want is not always so simple. Most pet shops have mongrel puppies, but if you can find one privately, perhaps through the local paper or the R.S.P.C.A., the chances of buying an infected animal are lessened. The weekly dog breeders' magazines, 'Our Dogs' and 'Dog World', list pedigree puppies for sale under breed headings. The Kennel Club will be able to tell you the name and address

Biting off more than they can chew?

English Setter pups

1

2

3

4

5

6

7

8

PHOTO QUIZ
Can you tell what these
puppies are going to be when
they grow up?
(Answers on page 141)

A cuddlesome trio

of the secretary of the club catering for the interests of the breed you have chosen, and this club should be able to furnish you with a list of reputable breeders. With highly fashionable or numerically small breeds you may have to book a puppy in advance. There are also dog dealing establishments supplying pedigree puppies, but you are more likely to get a fair deal going to a dog breeder rather than a middle man.

Recent American research has indicated that a puppy will adjust itself best to becoming a member of a new family if taken from its mother on the forty-ninth day after birth. In practice most puppies are not sold until they are eight weeks old, by which time they are fully weaned and completely independent. With a litter in a pet shop it is often difficult to know their age but many puppies are taken from their mothers too young and will need extra care if they are to survive succesfully.

Baby animals need frequent small meals and plenty of sleep, and young puppies are no exception. The puppy should have a bed of its own in a draught proof place. (Check at floor level with a lighted match.) The bed should be big enough for the dog to lie down flat, and a cardboard box that can be changed for a larger one as the puppy grows is quite adequate to start with. If bedding is used it should be easily replaceable or wash-able. Though provided with a warm, comfortable corner of their own, most puppies do not consider that this makes up for the absence of mother and litter mates, and they protest strongly for the first few nights because they are lonely. A wrapped hot water bottle and a loudly ticking clock may persuade the puppy that it has not been abandoned. When the surroundings have become familiar and the daily routine established this trouble disappears.

Puppies should be handled gently and firmly. A puppy falling from an adult's arms can injure itself badly. The best method of lifting is to put one hand under the chest between the forelegs, and use the other hand to support the hindquarters. Puppies should never be picked up by the front legs; and by the time they are eight weeks old, most are too heavy to like being picked up by the scruff of the neck.

Feeding should be of the best, given little and often. Four or five meals a day are the rule at eight weeks. The number of meals can be reduced to three at three months, though of course the quantity must be progressively increased. By six months the meals can be reduced to two, and at a year old a dog can have one meal only. In the early stages, two of the meals should be milk, with cereal or meal added, and two should be of minced or chopped meat. Any boneless meat is suitable, though dogs cannot digest too much fat or pork. Supplementary vitamins and minerals should be given to all growing animals, though they are not so essential for adults. There are at least two powders marketed which contain everything necessary and simplify adding the trace elements. The directions should be followed, as overdosing can be as harmful as

Two little Spaniels ready for a game

How to cool off on a hot day

However hard I scrub, I can't get the spots out

What have we here?

This young owner is very interested in learning about her dog's ear trouble as it is treated at a clinic of the People's Dispensary for Sick Animals

shortage. The amount of food given should be as much as the puppy will clear up with enthusiasm. Some pups are prepared to overeat and this is a point that must be judged by trial and error. When considering a dog's food it should be remembered that roughly two-thirds should be protein, that is meat, and the remainder can be made up of table scraps, biscuits, and so on.

Dog owners are liable to claim that their pets were house trained at a

Some dogs are
so enthusiastic about water...

... that you can't get
them out of the bath

With careful training
a puppy will learn to walk
at heel — and to ignore
other animals!

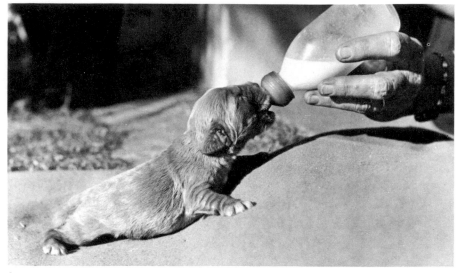

One puppy too many means hand rearing for the runt of the litter

Mother Alsation supervises dinner-time for her thirteen pups

fantastically early age, rather as some mothers boast about their children's progress. Some puppies learn faster than others and some owners put in more time and effort. An average pup should be house trained by day at four months or so, but may very well not be dry at night until six months old. Eight week old pups do not have very much bladder control and certainly cannot wait to go out. They will need to relieve themselves at least at two hourly intervals, and always after a meal, a sleep and an energetic play. Constant watchfulness on the owner's part is the quickest way to success. When the puppy pauses in its activity and starts to sniff the floor, it should be taken out immediately. Always stay with the puppy until it relieves itself and then praise it. Praise when it chooses the right spot is just as important as scolding when it chooses the wrong one. Puppies can be trained to use newspaper and this often simplifies the early morning cleaning up. However, with a dog that is trained to use newspaper, the family too has to be trained not to drop the Sunday papers on the floor until they have finished reading them.

Inoculations for puppies are a must before they meet other dogs or are taken to places where other dogs have been. Protection against distemper and hardpad, hepatitis and leptospiral infections can be obtained by a single injection, with later booster shots as advised by your veterinary surgeon. All these diseases are common and infectious, and will either prove lethal or will seriously undermine health and shorten a dog's life. Inoculations are usually given at three months, but if you feel you cannot wait that long before taking your puppy out, then it can be done at eight weeks and again at twelve.

All puppies need to be wormed in order to get rid of round worms, intestinal parasites that can affect a dog's condition. A responsible breeder will have wormed the puppies before selling them, but they should be done again at four months old. Roundworm tablets are on the market for dogs and the dosage recommended should be followed. Most puppies have roundworms. Some show no signs of them, while others pass them in the faeces or vomit them up. Roundworms are so called because they are round in section. They look like yellowish string, three to four inches long and pointed at both ends.

Puppies need a lot of sleep and it is a good idea to shut them up for an hour or so in the middle of the day. This not only enables them to get a rest but accustoms them to being left on their own. No puppy should be urged to play when it wants to rest, nor should it ever be teased. Long walks should be avoided until the animal is more than six months old, and then introduced gradually. Provided they are not over tired, the more puppies are taken about before this the better. Meeting people and traffic when young does a lot to produce a confident adult. Coaxing a puppy on a collar and lead for a short distance is a much easier job than doing the same thing for the first time with a half-grown animal. For a puppy that is car sick, perseverance with very short daily trips will often effect a cure. Preventing bad habits from forming is more important at this early stage of a dog's life than any formal training, which can safely be left until it is older.

Daily grooming with a soft brush should take place from the start. This enables fleas to be detected before they become too numerous, and small skin troubles to be seen and treated. Bathing is best left until the dog is adult, and dry cleaning powders should be used instead.

Puppies lose their milk teeth at about four months of age. Most teethe without any trouble but a few appear rather off-colour. Chewing is a necessity for young dogs. An uncooked marrow bone or one of the excellent cowhide toys sold for dogs should be provided for the exercise. Really dangerous things like stones small enough to be swallowed, splintery objects and electric leads must be guarded against. However much care is taken, there is usually an inevitable wastage of socks, bath sponges and other small portable objects during this stage of a puppy's life.

Finally it should perhaps be mentioned that two puppies will amuse each other and help bring each other up. They are roughly three times as much work and six times as much fun!

'No more photographs'

What a splendid joke!

ANIMAL FRIENDSHIPS

Irish Wolfhound
washes orphaned piglet
with motherly care

Let me have a word in your ear

Two white furry friends

There's a fascinating programme on television tonight

Great Dane with two
lion cub friends

A koala goes for a ride
on his Alsatian friend's back
at the Lone Pine Sanctuary
in Queensland, Australia

Siesta time
for a happy family

This is a working
partnership as well as
friendship

Now listen, cat,
this mouse is my friend

Siamese kitten
and Pyrenean pup

Sometimes friends can
be too possessive

CARTOON DOGS

The words 'dog' and 'bitch' are terms of abuse in the English language. They reflect quite accurately man's attitude over the centuries to the canine underworld of curs, strays and scavengers that has always co-existed with more valued useful dogs. In the days when cruelty was more overt, many of these ownerless dogs must have been made more ferocious by sadistic treatment. Not only were they feared for themselves but the cry of 'mad dog' brought with it the terror of rabies. Dogs were scavengers, eaters of any filth that was going. Dogs performed in public acts which polite society thought should be done in private. With this weight of public opinion against them, it is not suprising that the few dogs used in political cartoons before the turn of the century should have been used to vilify the characters they were meant to portray.

In the twentieth century everything changed. Dogs were no longer particularly feared, nor could they even be regarded as particularly useful. The fidelity of a dog for its master was no longer a cause for sentiment, for sentiment was out of fashion. The dog's desire to please could be regarded with affectionate amusement. The dog had become a bit of a buffoon and the cartoon dog became big business.

Though not the first, undoubtedly the most famous cartoon dog was Walt Disney's Pluto. He was the prototype for a whole series of lovable, longeared, stupid mutts. Quite what kind of dog Pluto is seems rather vague. Just plain 'hound dog' seems the best description. Like most modern cartoon dogs Pluto's intentions were always good, though alas his plans were always accident prone and his courage non-existent. Other hound dogs have followed him. Hanna-Barbera's Huckleberry Hound and Precious Pup both show more resourcefulness, and the latter is permitted a delightful snigger at the villain's discomfiture. Terry Toon Productions' Deputy Dawg is in the same genre, while Snoopy in Peanuts probably has as many fans as Pluto had in his heyday. Snoopy does not suffer so many physical catastrophes as Pluto did. He is shown day-dreaming the fantasies that always end in disaster.

A larger, corpulent and more formidable hound dog has been appearing in television advertisements for Kennomeat. This animal turns the tables on the human race by patronising his little man. Large dogs, like Marmaduke in the Evening News, are no longer shown or regarded as ferocious brutes. Rather it is their cumbersome size and shape that precipitate awkward situations for their cartoon owners. The only time that modern cartoon dogs are allowed to show their teeth is when they

Walt Disney's Pluto, the most famous of the cartoon dogs

© United Feature Syndicate, Inc. 1950 SCHULZ.

"See? I TOLD you it was a dog!"

"He isn't much protection, but what a conversation piece!"

"We've had him since he was only THIS high!"

are protecting the weak. Chopper, a caricature of a Bulldog created by Hanna-Barbera, deals out the most summary justice to the fox who is always threatening the life of the duckling Yacky Doodle.

Another cartoon type is the hairy, enigmatic beast, as sometimes drawn by Fotis in the Evening Standard. This type of dog, under its concealing curtain of hair, appears to be nursing a number of neuroses. Boot who accompanies The Perishers in the Daily Mirror is constantly worried, and Dougal in The Magic Roundabout also seems unsure of the role he wants to play in life. The Colonel in Disney's '101 Dalmations' was also the fussy type, though equipped with the standard heart of gold and a strong maternal instinct.

Surprisingly the terrier type of dog has played little part in cartoons. The hero of 'Lady and The Tramp' might perhaps qualify as a mongrel terrier, and certainly Lady had a Scottie friend with an impeccable Aberdeen accent. Other than that there is Bandit who figures in Hanna-Barbera's Johnny Quest adventures. Bandit typifies the terrier image of much courage encompassed in a small frame.

Cartoon dogs such as the Great Dane, Marmaduke, and Schultz's Snoopy
have a devoted following of fans. The Colonel,
plodding through the snow, is from Disney's '101 Dalmations'.

Answers to Photo Quiz on page 121
1. Bull Terriers
2. Pomeranians
3. Pekinese
4. Labradors
5. Alsatians
6. Samoyed
7. Bulldog
8. Jack Russell Terrier

ACKNOWLEDGMENTS

Associated Newspapers 127 B; British Museum 79 B, 98 L; Wendy Boorer 80 R; James Buchanan & Company Limited 112 B; Camera Clix 4, 13, 81 B, 123, 130, 131; C. M. Cooke & Son 18, 40 B, 42 R, 43 TL, 43 BL, 44 TL, 44 B, 45 T, 45 BL, 46 TL, 46 TR, 46 B, 52 TR, 53 B, 74 B, 89 B; Camera Press 22, 121 BL; Cruft's Dog Show Society 113; Crown copyright, by permission of the Controller of H.M.S.O. 114 R; Daily Express 126 L; Walt Disney Productions Ltd 136, 138 BR; John Freeman 77, 81 T; Fleetway Studio 80 L; Farmers Weekly 106 BR; C.A.W. Guggisberg 25; The Gramophone Company Limited 112 T; Hamlyn Group Library 76 R, 95 R; Imperial Chemical Industries 117; Incorporated Press of Great Britain Ltd 138 TR, 138 CL, 138 BL; Russ Kinne 26; Kobal Collection 68 B; London Museum 60 TL, 60 TR; Luciana's Photos 8, 69 T; Larousse 76 L; Metropolitan Museum of Art, Rogers Fund, 1940 74 T; Mustograph 78 B, 111, 114 B, 116 T, 116 B; Mansell 88 T, 98 R; Novosti Press Agency 69 B; Antichità della Campania, Naples 96; Odhams Syndication 16 TR, 16 B, 59; Pictorial Press 17, 28, 34, 36 R, 50 TR, 61, 63, 75 T, 78 T, 102, 104 TL, 104 TR, 104 BL, 109 B, 118, 120, 124 BL, 125 T, 125 B, 126 TR, 132 B, 140; Photographic Library of Australia 27; Popperfoto 91 T, 91 C, 92, 95 L; Radio Times Hulton Picture Library 11, 12, 30-1, 37, 58 T, 62 B, 66-7, 71, 75 B, 82 T, 86, 88 B, 89 T, 89 C, 90-1 B and endpapers, 105 B, 106 BL; Royal Academy of Arts 60 BL; Leonard Lee Rue III 20; R.S.P.C.A. 101 L; Syndication International 10, 16 TL, 19 L, 19 R, 33, 36 L, 50 TL, 50 BL, 51, 52 TL, 53 T, 54, 56, 58 B, 60 BR, 62 T, 64, 65, 68 TL, 68 TR, 70, 72, 79 T, 82 B, 83, 94, 99 T, 99 B, 100 T, 101 R, 105 TL, 105 TR, 106 TL, 106 TR, 108 TL, 109 T, 114 TL, 121 except BL and CR, 122, 124 TL, 124 TR, 126 BR, 127 T, 128, 129, 132 T, 133 T, 133 B, 134, 135 T, 135 B, 139; Saxone, Lilley & Skinner 110, 115 L; Spillers Limited 115 R; Sally Anne Thompson 14, 15, 32, 35, 38, 40 TL, 40 TR, 41 L, 41 R, 42 L, 43 TR, 43 C, 43 BR, 44 TR, 45 BR, 47, 48, 50 BR, 52 B, 55 B, 85, 90 T, 121 CR; Topix 93, 108 BR; John Topham 100 B, 107 L, 107 R; John Tarlton 108 BL; United Feature Syndicate, Inc. 138; Joe Van Wormer 23, 24; Michael Wright 55 T; Guy Withers 84; Western Mercury & Somerset Herald 124 BR.